MANSFIELD'S TRAMS

By
Tony Hurst

Car no.10, built in 1905, and still in original condition, stands in the Sutton Road depot yard in 1930. Adjacent is one of the single deck buses operated by the company in the 1920s. Photograph Dr. H. Nichol, copyright NTM.

To the memory of my father, the late Robert Edgar Hurst, a Mansfield man born and bred; also to the memory of Maurice J. O'Connor, the Mansfield lawyer who tirelessly recorded the tramway scene in Mansfield and elsewhere.

ACKNOWLEDGEMENTS

One of the great pleasures of researching a history of this type comes from corresponding with and meeting so many different people from so many different walks of life. I would like to acknowledge the help and assistance given by the following individuals and organisations, not in any particular order. Any conclusions I may have reached in the light of incomplete evidence are my own and I accept full responsibility for them.

The late Reg Cooke of Mansfield, Ian and Alan Halfpenny of Mansfield, Mrs G Hooks of Mansfield, N Shiels of Mansfield, Maisie Strauther of Mansfield, the late Arthur Hurst of Mansfield, Barrs of Mansfield, Mrs J Sheldon of Mansfield Woodhouse, Paul Atchinson, photographer of Eastwood, Keith Romig of Leyton, A Eric Old of Bangor, Rosy Thacker of the National Tramway Museum, Glynn Wilton ditto, Richard Wiseman of the Light Rail Transit Association and Dr Bob Tebb, both formerly at The Brunts Grammar School, Mansfield, which was my old school, Michael Taplin of the LRTA, A D Packer of Bromley, Roy Brook, John Gillham, Richard Petrie on behalf of Mrs M O'Connor, Geoff Lumb, Mr Kennedy of the Ulster Folk Museum, Colin Brown of Luton, David Beilby of Oldham, Mrs Barbara Gallon, Old Mansfield Society, Victoria Barlow and all the staff at Mansfield Museum, David Ottewell of Eakring, Notts, John Andrews of Cardiff, Ms J E Franks of Mansfield District Council Chief Executive Office, A J Gordon, Notts County Council District Librarian, Edgar Jordan of Reading, Philip Cartwright, Stagecoach East Midlands, Trent Buses, Adam Gordon of Chetwode, Bucks, David Crute and staff at Mansfield Library, Mrs Hastings and staff, Sutton in Ashfield Library, Jeremy Plews and Roger Grayson, Mansfield Chad, E B H Chappell, Alan Mills and Patrick Lidgett, The Omnibus Society, Gordon Fairchild, Peacehaven, E Sussex, G L Griffiths, Swansea, John Wells, Photographics of Lowestoft, The late John

H Price, B Lund, Recollections of a Bygone Age, Ian Yearsley of the Tramway Museum Society and Roads and Road Transport History Conference, The Kithead Trust, F P Groves of Keyworth, Mrs Stoddart, Asst Archivist, Leics Records Office, BBC Woman's Hour, Godfrey Croughton, Transport Ticket Society, Balfour Beatty, Staff at Notts County Council Archives Office, Dorothy Petrie, Local Studies Library, Nottingham. I am particularly indebted to Bob Tebb for undertaking the proof reading and acknowledge that I did not always take his advice!

With regard to Chapter 10, 'On the Trams' this was taken from a transcript of a tape recording made by the late Mr Eric Evans in 1983. I have been unable to trace the holder of the copyright for this, despite diligent enquiries. I wish therefore to place on record my acknowledgement of the work done by the originator and also express my sincere thanks to the Officers of the National Tramway Museum, Mansfield Library, Mansfield Museum and Nottingham Central Library for their assistance in these enquiries.

The extract from D H Lawrence's 'Tickets Please' is reproduced by kind permission of Laurence Pollinger Ltd and the estate of Freida Lawrence Ravagli.

I also wish to place on record my appreciation of the research done by the late Maurice J O'Connor in to the history of Mansfield trams before his untimely death in 1995.

Also my thanks to the Editor and staff of the Mansfield 'Chad' newspaper for allowing my use of their extensive archives of letters and photographs, from which a great deal of the content of this book has been gleaned.

Finally, my thanks to Vicky for encouraging me to complete the research and assisting me to meet the deadlines. To anyone I may have missed, I apologise but tender my grateful thanks anyway.

Cover photographs. Two of Mansfield's doubledecker trams loading in the Market Place, Mansfield in 1930. Both photos M.J. O'Connor and Dr. Nicol, copyright National Tramway Museum.

CONTENTS

PREFACE

My father was born in Mansfield before the First World War and I was born in Sutton in Ashfield before the Second. By the time I arrived on the scene the electric trams between those two towns had made their final journey. However, my father knew them well and it was his anecdotes that first aroused my interest in the trams. He was born in a small terraced house, now demolished, in Herbert Street, off Stockwell Gate Hill which was until fairly recent times a narrow steep road with a high stone wall on the south side behind which stood the once dreaded No.105, Stockwell Gate, the Union Workhouse.

On the opposite side stood streets of small terraced houses and pubs, including Herbert Street. As the trams slowly descended the gradient, they were liable to run over obstructions allegedly placed on the tracks by the brothers Hurst. My father used to say they put pennies on the line to be bent by the passing trams, and my uncle, his brother, recently confided in me that my father, being the 'clever dick' of the family had made up small explosive devices which he placed on the tracks, to the alarm and consternation of the drivers of passing trams and also presumably, the passengers.

These family tales I take with a pinch of salt. There was little cash to spare in those days for working class families to lay their precious pennies on the tram line, for the doubtful pleasure of having them made worthless by passing trams, nor for purchasing the necessary ingredients for explosive devices. That such pranks were played is well known, indeed we read that in 1916, a local youth was fined 15 shillings for placing colliery detonators on the tram lines and no doubt my father and his brothers liked to pretend to each other that they were the perpetrators of such pranks.

So my interest in tramways was kindled and my father, realising my interest, suggested that I might like to take up an apprenticeship with the Brush Electrical Engineering Company at nearby Loughborough, once well known for the manufacture of many fine tramcars. However by this time I wished to assert my independence and went instead into the aircraft industry where I spent most of my spare time making model trams (and still do!)

I therefore rather belatedly dedicate this book to the memory of my father and also to that of Maurice O'Connor, the Mansfield lawyer and later a founder member and director of the National Tramway Museum at Crich, Derbyshire, who tirelessly recorded the tramway scene in Mansfield and elsewhere, and to whom tramway enthusiasts like myself will be for ever grateful.

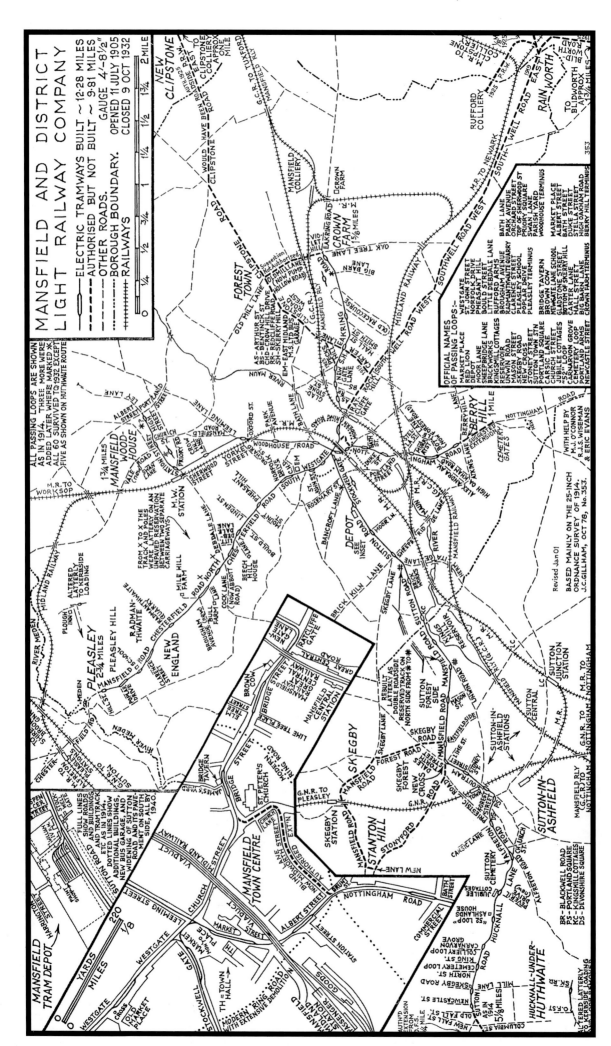

MANSFIELD AND DISTRICT LIGHT RAILWAY COMPANY

ELECTRIC TRAMWAYS BUILT ~ 12·28 MILES
AUTHORISED BUT NOT BUILT ~ 9·81 MILES
OTHER ROADS.
BOROUGH BOUNDARY.
RAILWAYS

GAUGE 4′-8½″
OPENED 11 JULY 1905
CLOSED 9 OCT 1932

ALL PASSING LOOPS ARE SHOWN AS IN 1914. THREE MORE WERE ADDED LATER WHERE MARKED ✳. ALL 60 SURVIVED TO 1932 EXCEPT FIVE AS SHOWN ON HUTHWAITE ROUTE.

BASED MAINLY ON THE 25-INCH ORDNANCE SURVEY OF 1914. No.353.
J.C.GILLHAM, OCT 78, No.353.
WITH HELP BY M.J. O'CONNOR R.J.S. WISEMAN & ERIC EVANS
Revised Jan 01

OFFICIAL NAMES OF PASSING LOOPS:-

WESTGATE
ST. JOHN STREET
NORFOLK DRIVE
PHEASANT HILL
MARKET PLACE
RED LION
MOOR LANE
LITTLE DEBDALE LANE
DEPOT
BRICKWORKS LANE
RUFFORD ARMS
BROUGHAM AVENUE
RADMANTHWAITE QUARRY
KINGSMILL COTTAGES
CLARENCE STREET
UNWIN ROAD
MASON STREET
RESERVOIR
POPLAR DRIVE
NEW CROSS
STONEY STREET
SUTTON TOWN STN
PORTLAND SQUARE
JUBILEE COTTAGES
CHURCH STREET
"52" LOOP
CARNARVON GROVE
CEMETERY LOOP
BROAD LANE
NEWCASTLE STREET

BRIDGE TAVERN
BRIMWELL COTTAGE
NEWCASTLE LANE SCHOOL
GLADSTONE STREET
BOTTOM OF SKERRY HILL
CARTER LANE
HALL STREET
HIGH OAKHAM ROAD
CROWN FARM TERMINUS

MARKET PLACE
ALBERT STREET
BATH STREET
DUKE STREET
BATH LANE
PARK AVENUE
ORCHARD STREET
TOP OF SHERWOOD ST
PRIORY SQUARE
SWAN LANE
PARISH YARD
WOODHOUSE TERMINUS
HIGH OAKHAM ROAD
BERRY HILL TERMINUS

BR - BLACKWELL ROAD
PS - PORTLAND SQUARE
KC - KINGSMILL COTTAGES
DS - DEVONSHIRE SQUARE

AS - ARTHUR ST
BS - BENTINCK ST
CH - CROW HILL DRIVE
RR - REDCLIFFE ROAD
SH - SKERRY HILL
EM - EAST MIDLAND
M.S.LTD BUS GARAGE

TH = TOWN HALL

Chapter 1
History

Just over one hundred years ago Mansfield was described as a compact stone built market town of some 12,000 inhabitants, serving an essentially agricultural neighbourhood. Things were to change with the opening of several collieries in the area and with the granting of a Charter of Incorporation as a Borough in 1891 the population rapidly expanded. The need for some form of transport more efficient than the old horse brakes and carriers' carts became pressing. Up until then, horse-drawn wagonettes connected the town with its outlying districts and racing between opposing owners vying for patronage often reached dangerous levels.

In 1898, a number of the town's businessmen joined in the formation of a company with the title of 'The Mansfield Motor Car Co' with a share capital of £5,000, with the object of providing mechanised transport for surrounding villages and towns not served by the lines of the Midland or Great Northern Railways. Mr William Jackson Chadburn of whom more later, was one of the directors, together with Charles Manners, F A Robinson the foundry owner, G A Fish and R F Vallance the Borough Surveyor. F Hameyer was the Company Secretary. They purchased a steam bus appropriately named 'The Pioneer' from the Liquid Fuel Engineering Co of Cowes, Isle of Wight. This was successfully driven to Mansfield and a service commenced linking the outlying towns and villages with the town. Unfortunately problems with the tyres caused this enterprise to be abandoned within a few months.

Mr Chadburn and his fellow directors did not allow this setback to diminish their determination to see a modern public transport system in Mansfield for in November 1898, we see them making an application to the Light Railway Commissioners for an Order under the Light Railways Act of 1896: 'To authorise the Promoters to construct, work and use the hereinafter described Light Railways in the Parishes of Mansfield, Mansfield Woodhouse and Sutton in Ashfield, the borough of Mansfield and the Urban Districts of Mansfield Woodhouse and Sutton in Ashfield'.

The lines were proposed as follows: 'LINE No.1. 5 furlongs 9.25 chains in length commencing in Church Street Mansfield Woodhouse at a point opposite the north west corner of the building at the corner of Church Street and High Street and proceeding thence along Church Street, Church Hill and Mansfield Road and terminating at the boundary between the Parish of Mansfield Woodhouse and the Borough of Mansfield.

'LINE No.2. 6 furlongs 2.60 chains in length commencing in Mansfield Road by a junction with Line No.1, at its southern terminus as hereinbefore described and proceeding thence along Mansfield Road, Woodhouse Road, Leeming Street, the south east side of the Market Place, and Market Street, Mansfield, and terminating in the latter at a point 30 yards or thereabouts south of the north east corner of the Town Hall.

'LINE No.3. 7 furlongs 8.85 chains in length, commencing by a junction with Line No 2 hereinbefore described, at a point opposite the north corner of the building at the corner of the Market Place and Church Street, Mansfield, and proceeding thence along the north east side of the Market Place, West Gate and Chesterfield Road and terminating therein at a point 100 yards south east of the entrance to the private residence of Beech Hill.

Three young ladies at the controls of a Mansfield tram during the First World War. Their names are unknown and the author would be pleased to hear from anyone who may have knowledge of their identity. This photograph was probably used in a local newspaper campaign to recruit female drivers and conductors during the First World War. Photograph National Tramway Museum.

A bustling scene in Mansfield Market at the turn of the century. The trams had not yet arrived but road widening has commenced at the bottom of Leeming Street in preparation. Wilkinson's shop at the corner of Leeming Street and Market Place has been reduced from four bays to two and the buildings jutting out halfway up Leeming Street were soon to be demolished.

LINE No.4. 1 mile 4 furlongs 5.60 chains in length, commencing by a junction with Line No 3 hereinbefore described, at a point 25 yards or thereabouts south east of the east corner of the Market Place, Mansfield and West Gate and proceeding thence along the north west side of the Market Place, Stockwell Gate and Sutton Road and terminating in the latter at the boundary between the Borough of Mansfield and the Parish of Sutton in Ashfield.

'LINE No.5. 1 mile 5 furlongs 0.40 chains in length, commencing by a junction with Line No 4 at this terminus as hereinbefore described and proceeding thence along Sutton Road, Mansfield Road, Sutton, Outram Street and Portland Square, Sutton and terminating in the latter at a point opposite the east corner of the building at the corner of Fore Street and Idlewells.

The proposed lines were intended to be constructed to a gauge of 3ft 6ins using electric power, 'applied according to a system approved by the Board of Trade, or animal or any mechanical power other than steam power'. So, steam trams were specifically excluded.

A meeting of the Light Railway Commissioners under the Chairmanship of The Earl of Jersey

GCB was held at Mansfield Town Hall at the end of May 1900. There was some dispute with the representative for Mansfield Woodhouse over who would bear the cost of widening of roads.

The estimated costs of the five and three quarter miles of line proposed was £41,583 5s and for the electrical equipment £35,950, making a total of £77,533 5s. To meet this the company had fixed the capital at £100,000 of which one third would be issued as 6 per cent preference shares with the usual borrowing powers of one third of that amount.

A purchase clause, enabling the Local Authorities to purchase the undertaking after 30 years had been made. The Mansfield Corporation obtained an order enabling them to supply power to the undertaking and the usual provision was made for the maintenance of the public roadway either side of the tramway by the company. These proposals were supported by the Urban District of Sutton in Ashfield and also by the Borough of Mansfield in the person of their elected representative, Mr William Jackson Chadburn.

It may be pertinent at this point to ask why, if the Mansfield Corporation were such enthusiastic supporters and providers for the scheme, they did not undertake it themselves. The reason usually given is that Councils were

sometimes unwilling to ask ratepayers to foot the bill for construction and operation of tramways in case, as had happened elsewhere, they were to make a substantial loss. If the trams were to make a profit of course, there was the opportunity under the purchase clause for the council to compulsory buy the undertaking, although in this case this never happened. Instead the Council remained happily on the sidelines taking every opportunity to snipe at the company and criticise the service, particularly in the latter stages.

At the end of the hearing, the Light Railway Commissioners stated that in view of what they had heard they would be happy to recommend to the Board of Trade to grant the application.

In February 1901, the Company obtained powers under the Mansfield and District Light Railways Order of that year, to extend the line to Hucknall-under-Huthwaite, and to the borough and county boundary at Pleasley. They also obtained powers to alter the gauge of the proposed light railway from 3ft 6 inches to 4ft 8½ inches.

In 1902, the Nottinghamshire and Derbyshire Tramways Company made application for no less than 79 miles of route, which would have connected Mansfield with Blackwell, Swanwick, Ripley and Belper, a total of some 20 miles of single track with passing loops. There were proposed lines to Heanor, Ilkeston, Nottingham and ultimately Derby. Most of these proposals failed to materialise but a 15 mile long route was eventually constructed in 1913, connecting Ripley with Nottingham and known as "The Nottinghamshire and Derby Tramway Company". Meanwhile, The Mansfield company was finally incorporated on May 15th 1901 as the "Mansfield and District Light Railways Co."

Further powers were granted under the Mansfield and District Light Railway Order of 1903. Included in this order were powers to convey goods, parcels, minerals and animals in addition to passengers. The company hoped that minerals would be one of the most profitable features of the undertaking, particularly on the Hucknall under Huthwaite line.

On 20 April 1906, the company gave notice of their intention to purchase an electric locomotive and a number of trailers to convey domestic coal from the various mines adjacent to the tramway. The intention was for the locomotive to draw six braked trailers of 10 tons capacity each, attended by two brakesmen. The Board of Trade were in agreement with these proposals, except that they specified that only four trailers should be drawn.

However, on receiving a copy of the proposals, the Mansfield Corporation sent to the company and to the Board of Trade, a letter objecting most strongly, on the grounds of danger and annoyance to the public likely to be caused by loaded trains of coal proceeding through the streets of Mansfield at all hours. In the light of subsequent events one cannot help but have some sympathy for the fears expressed in this letter. However, on 14 May 1906 the company solicitor Mr Arthur T Ashwell, replying to the Town Clerk Mr John Harrop White, said in his letter, 'I cannot help thinking that your Corporation do not fully understand what my clients' proposals really are. It is not the intention of the company to haul loads of coal through the streets at all hours of the night, nor to do anything which might be a source of danger or annoyance to the public.'

The proposals did not go ahead, according to the minutes, 'due to difficulties with capital expenditure and representations form His Grace, the Duke of Portland.' The Duke was a powerful force in those days and his representations were obviously taken seriously by the company, for shortly after the proposals for hauling coal through the streets were quietly withdrawn, we read that His Grace had been pleased to permit the extension of the tramway into Mansfield Woodhouse by way of the New Road which was being constructed on the Duke's estate.

Further extensions were authorised by the Mansfield and District Light Railways (Extensions) Order of 1907. This order gave the company powers to construct a line from the Market Square along Church Street, Bridge Street, Ratcliffe Gate, Newgate Lane, Skerry Hill and the Eakring Road to a point at the Mansfield borough boundary known as Crown Farm.

Mansfield Colliery, opened in 1905, was situated at Crown Farm, and was to become one of the biggest collieries in the country with an annual output of over 1,000,000 tons. Naturally getting colliers to and from work was an important source of income for the tramway company.

Another line was authorised along Skegby Road to Skegby Station (GNR) and then along the Teversal Road, returning in a loop by way of Stoneyford Road, to Sutton. This line would have provided transport for miners at the Sutton, Teversal and Silverhill collieries. Difficulties with the line to Mansfield Woodhouse, and the extension to Crown Farm exhausted the Company financially. The Skegby line was continuously postponed and eventually the powers lapsed.

Further powers were granted under the 1907 Order for an extension from the Hucknall-under-Huthwaite terminus as far as Common Road, where a depot was to be constructed. These powers were later taken over by the Notts and Derbys Tramways Co. and eventually lapsed.

A further line was authorised from Albert Street on the Nottingham Road route, along Dark Lane (now Midworth Street) and Church Lane, to Bridge Street, to join the proposed line to Crown Farm. This was, and still is, a very narrow thoroughfare and, unable to come to terms with the trustees of the adjoining properties, the idea was given up.

The 'Pioneer' steam omnibus which operated in Mansfield in 1898. Purchased from East Cowes on the Isle of Wight where the author served his apprenticeship in aircraft engineering, the vehicle had seats for 22 passengers and pulled a trailer with an equal number of seats. Unfortunately, the tyres could not be persuaded to stay on the wheels and the enterprise folded within the space of a few months. The remains of the 'Pioneer' were still to be found behind the present museum building in the 1930s. Photograph Mansfield Museum.

Track laying in Westgate about 1905. Photograph Mansfield Museum.

Chapter 2
Construction of the Lines

Although nominally a light railway system, the line was constructed entirely using ordinary tramway methods. Having Mansfield as its centre, lines radiated out from the Market Place northwards to Pleasley, westward to Sutton in Ashfield and Huthwaite (called Hucknall under Huthwaite in those days), south along Nottingham Road to the Mansfield Urban District boundary at Berry Hill Lane and in a north easterly direction they served the urban district of Mansfield Woodhouse. Other lines were proposed to Crown Farm, Skegby and Teversal but in the event only the first of these was ever built. The line thus served several urban districts and was in effect truly 'inter-urban'.

A total of 12.28 miles of tramway was built to the standard gauge of 4ft 8½ inches, with a further 9.81 miles authorised but never built. The system was laid out as a single track with passing places arranged at various distances depending on the nature of the route, the idea being to have one passing place within sight of the next. So states an early engineer's report, but this was not always possible and occasionally trams met each other on single sections of the track. The route was considered to be an easy one by Messrs. Bramwell and Harris of London, the consulting engineers. The steepest gradient was 1 in 16 and the sharpest curve of 50 foot radius. This was before the opening of the Crown Farm route with its 1 in 10 gradient on the notorious Skerry Hill.

The rails used were 90lb per yard in weight and 45 feet long, the general specification being to section 1 of the British Standard. All the rails and fishplates were supplied by Bolckow, Vaughan and Co. of Middlesbrough. The track was laid on a bed of concrete six inches thick, composed of 1 part Portland Cement (supplied by the Associated Cement Co) to 6 of aggregate. Under all joints, Ames Bulldog anchor sole plates were used. No intermediate anchors were put in 'except in one or two special cases'.

Electrical bonding was carried out with 'Neptune' type solid copper bonds, described as 'oooo B&S bonds', supplied by the United Steel Products Co. Two were used at every rail joint and one cross bond every 40 yards. In addition there was at least one cross bond at every passing place, supplied by R W Blackwell and Co Ltd.

The points were 10ft 6ins long and 100 foot radius and together with the 1 in 5 angled crossings were supplied by Hadfield's Steel Foundry of Sheffield. The standard paving consisted of a row of 6 inch by 3 inch granite setts on both sides of the rails, the space between the rails being filled with tarmacadam. At points and crossings and in the centre of Mansfield, the granite sett paving was carried right across to 18 inches outside the rails. The granite setts were of course extremely hard wearing

Laying the tracks to Mansfield Woodhouse in Leeming Street in June 1906. All the buildings on the right-hand side of the street are new, the old ones having been recently demolished during the widening of Leeming Street. The sign says, rather quaintly, 'Road Stopped'. Nowadays 'Road Closed' signs are all too familiar. The police officer remains on his post but as traffic is much lighter with the road being 'stopped', he finds time for a chat with a passer-by. No doubt he was kept fairly busy advising travellers of the alternative route. Photograph Mansfield Museum.

and the tramway company, being made responsible by the provisions of the Tramways Act 1870 for the upkeep of the road surface up to 18 inches outside the rails, found this method of paving the most suitable.

The hollow side of the rails was filled with a cement fillet to which the granite setts were butted. The granite setts were supplied by A and F Manuelle and the Mount Sorrell Granite company and were laid on a bed of sand grouted in with cement.

The overhead electrical equipment was carried on side poles with bracket arms 12 or 16 feet in length, although in narrow streets metal plates known as rosettes were used, on the front of buildings. The trolley wire was supported 21 feet above the track. The poles were of three sizes, 840lb, 960lb and 1168lb, supplied by Stewarts and Lloyds of Glasgow and Birmingham. The pole bases, columns and finials were supplied by the Railway and General Engineering Co Ltd of Nottingham.

The trolley wire was double throughout and was of hard drawn copper, from the National Conduit and Cable Co. It came in continuous lengths of half a mile from section insulator to section insulator and was generally fed at both ends of every section. Flexible suspension was used throughout. The straight line 'ears' (the part the overhead wire was clamped to) were 15 inches long and on curves, 24 inches long. All were made of gunmetal, grooved to fit the trolley wire. All the ears were supplied by the Electric Tramway Equipment Co. The guard wire consisted of galvanised mild steel stranded cable, earthed at every fifth pole by a connecting wire soldered to the guard and riveted to the post. The guard wire was supplied by F Smith and Co of Halifax. All the posts were bonded to the rails by a copper bond.

Cables were laid on the solid system from the depot to the various section pillars. Telephone and test wires were carried overhead, the three wires supported on insulators fixed to the poles. The section boxes were supplied to the company by the Callender Cable and Construction Co. The system was earthed at the junction of the different lines in Mansfield Market Place and leads were run back to the depot where they were connected to the recording instruments on the switchboard.

According to driver Eric Evans, this had the disadvantage that if more than one car tried to climb Stockwell Gate hill at one time, the breaker would blow under the Town Hall and a duty electrician had to be sent from the depot to reset it. At busy times it was not unusual to see several cars queuing at the Red Lion loop waiting to ascend Stockwell Gate hill.

Electricity was supplied by Mansfield Corporation Electricity Department at 550 volts. The company paid 1¾d for the first 250,000 units and 1½d thereafter. The switchboard at the depot was made by Berry, Skinner and Co; it consisted of seven panels and a negative booster arranged as follows:

Three controlled incoming Corporation feed lines, fitted with reverse current circuit breakers, ammeters, switches and BTH integrated watt-hour meters; two line feeder panels with standard equipment;
One 'Board of Trade' panel;
One negative booster panel.

The contracts for the permanent way and electrical equipment was carried out by J G White and Co under the supervision of Mr A Carlton-Blythe. The Callender Cable and Construction Co supplied and laid the cable work as sub-contractors to J G White and Co. Mr Charles Robert Walker was the resident engineer and was appointed general manager and secretary of the tramway when it opened.

During the construction of the line constant complaint was received from the Mansfield Town Council. In a letter dated 26 April 1904, signed by the Town Clerk Mr John Harrop White, the Town Council made the following complaints about the construction work:

'1. The posts are placed irregularly on either side of the road without any apparent reason, on the grounds of appearance alone this is very objectionable. Where posts are used they should be on one side of the road.

'2. Three posts are placed on the Market Square at the north end; these should be dispensed with.

'3. The design of the posts is poor and should be improved.

'4. Posts are shown throughout the total length of the line. In narrow streets the posts will prove objectionable and brackets or attachments to the walls of houses should be substituted.

'5. The tar macadam is not strong enough.

'6. The rail joints do not butt up close but have a space of a thirty-second of an inch. The rails are joined by fishplates only; this is not sufficient. Adequate anchor plates ... should be provided, otherwise, most probably in a few years, bumping will take place, cars will oscillate and smooth running will be impossible. [prophetic words!]

7. The points are shown to be 7 foot 6 inches long, these should be longer, say 12 foot 6 inches.

'8. It is impossible for the promoter to begin Railway No.7 until Albert Street has been widened.'

How many of these complaints were taken up by the company is not known, however we do know that the widening of Albert Street was not completed to the satisfaction of the Board of Trade Inspectors on the opening day, and a service could not be provided to Nottingham Road until the necessary remedial work had been carried out.

While the trams were being assembled in the roadway, work was going ahead inside the depot to try to get the tracks and buildings completed. This view, possibly taken from the top deck of a tramcar outside the depot, shows the tracks being laid in the depot yard on Sutton Road in 1905. Photograph Mansfield Museum.

Chapter 3
The First Tramcars

For the opening of the system in 1905 twelve open top four wheel cars were provided by Hurst Nelson and Co Ltd of Motherwell, Scotland. These were followed in 1906 by six top-covered four wheel cars from the Brush Electrical Engineering Co of Loughborough. Apart from the top covers on the latter, the cars were similar in specification. This has led to some incorrect speculation in the past that all these cars were provided by Hurst, Nelson and Co and that the top covers were supplied later by Brush for Nos.13 to 18.

The electrical equipment was provided by the British Westinghouse Co, the motors being of their No.200 type. These had a draw bar pull of 1,250lb, a nominal 25hp, each car having two motors. The controllers were of the Westinghouse Type 90. The wheels were 30 inch diameter with steel tyres and with 500 volts on the motor terminals the cars were designed to operate at a speed of approximately 10mph. They were capable of carrying 50% overload for short periods without undue heating or sparking. This capability was severely tested on occasions as we shall

read later. All cars had hand operated brakes on all four wheels and in addition, a Newell Magnetic Track Brake operated by the controller.

The trolley heads were provided by Brecknell, Munro and Rogers Ltd and R W Blackwell and Co. The destination blinds were the familiar 'Acme' rollers. These were replaced in later years by destination boards carried on the sides of the cars.

The Hurst, Nelson cars were fitted with HN 21E trucks and the Brush cars with Brush AA types. The wheelbase in both cases was 6 feet. The other principal dimensions of the cars were as follows:

Length over fenders : 27 feet
Length over platforms: 26 feet
Length of body outside: 15 feet
Width over pillars : 6 feet 6 inches
Height inside: 6 feet 9 inches
Height of lower saloon over rail level: 9 feet 9 inches
Seating capacity: 22 lower, 25 upper

Hudson, Bowring lifeguards were fitted to all cars. The cost of the Brush cars was £620 each and when the Mansfield Railway constructed its bridge over Nottingham Road in 1916,

the Brush cars were found to be too high to pass under, so were henceforth barred from this route. The height of this bridge was 16ft 3ins.

When the Hurst, Nelson cars were delivered, the depot on Sutton Road was not ready so the cars were simply assembled in the roadway. This involved matching up the bodies with the trucks and motors then assembling the top deck and erecting the trolley poles. The completed cars were then stored in a shed on Chesterfield Road until the depot was ready. The site of this shed is now occupied by St Philip Neri Roman Catholic church. It is interesting to try to visualise the disassembled cars travelling down by train from Scotland, being unloaded in the Midland Railway goods yard and then dragged through the streets on rollers by teams of horses.

In 1908 the opportunity arose to obtain two nearly new cars from the Cavehill and Whitewell Tramway, a line operating on the outskirts of Belfast and, like the Mansfield company, engineered by J G White & Co. This line was opened in 1882 as a roadside steam tramway, but the steam locomotives were so unreliable

Open top Hurst, Nelson built car No.1 adjacent to St Marks Church in Nottingham Road about 1906. From a hand coloured postcard, courtesy Mansfield Museum.

that they were later replaced by horses. In 1906 the line was reconstructed in the middle of the road and electrified. Three miles long, it was separated by a matter of a few feet from the lines of the Belfast Corporation at their respective termini. The Belfast Corporation attempted on several occasions to gain control of the Cavehill and Whitewell company which resisted in spirited fashion. The company even applied for an order to enable them to run their own trams over the Corporation tracks into the city centre.

The Cavehill and Whitewell company purchased five open top four wheel double deck cars from Brush in 1905 and five in 1906. They were powered by two BTH 25hp motors, the first five fitted with Brush's own design of radial truck, the 'AA' type and the 1906 batch with Lycett and Conaty radial trucks. They all had four windows in each saloon side and were of sturdy construction, with the 1906 batch able to seat 72 passengers. The overall length was 32 feet 6 inches and the length over the body 20 feet, on a 9ft wheelbase.

The Cavehill company soon realised that they had been over-generous in their estimate of the number of cars required to operate the service and in 1908 disposed of two of them to the Mansfield company through the offices of J G White and Co. These became Nos.19 and 20 in the Mansfield fleet and are believed to have been fitted with Lycett and Conaty radial trucks.

These were later replaced by Peckham P22 types. Meanwhile, back in Belfast, the Corporation finally managed to gain control of the Cavehill line in 1910 and rebuilt the remaining 8 cars to look and behave as much like the Belfast standard cars as possible. Most of them remained in service until the closure of the Belfast Tramways in 1954.

The two cars arrived in Mansfield with a livery of light green and cream which was in contrast to the red and cream of the Mansfield Company. The green and cream became the house colours of Balfour, Beatty and Co and all the Mansfield trams were eventually repainted in these colours.

Before the main orders for the cars had been placed in 1905, the following letter had been sent from the company's solicitors, Messrs. Bramwell and Harris, to the Town Clerk of Mansfield, the redoubtable John Harrop White, on 8 December 1904:

'Dear Sir
Re Mansfield and District Light Railway – Tram Cars.

Before ordering the cars we would be glad to consider any comments or suggestions your council might put forward. If they have a preference for any particular style or type of car we will do everything possible to give effect to their wishes.'

We do not have the reply to this courteous letter, but a press report indicates that the new cars were to be 'of the Nottingham type' which may have been the Corporation's suggestion.

In addition to the above, an order was placed in 1905 for a car combining the duties of water car and snow plough. This car was delivered by the Brush Electrical Co, the following year. We have no details of this car, but we may assume it was in every way similar to the one delivered to nearby Chesterfield by the Brush Company the same year.

Car No.13 poses with its crew at the Mansfield Woodhouse terminus in 1907. Noticeable in this photograph is the folding gate to prevent unauthorised entry on to the front platform, also the metal supports at each end of the top deck to hold up the balconies. Perhaps the manufacturers, Brush Electrical Engineering Co of Loughborough, had heard of the overcrowding on Mansfield's trams and wanted to ensure their balconies could stand the strain! Photograph Mansfield Museum.

Chapter 4
The Tramway Opens

Progress for the first two or three years seems to have been fairly slow. These were boom years for tramway equipment manufacturers and many found themselves snowed under with orders. Many undertakings had to look abroad for such essential items as steel rails and electrical equipment. And there was always the problem of finance, with such undertakings finding themselves in competition for what money there was available. In 1903 the Mansfield Company had to sell out most of its shares to London and foreign financiers to raise the necessary capital.

Track laying finally commenced in January 1905. According to the *Mansfield Advertiser*, the probability was *'that the work will start at the limits of the lines, leaving the laying of the lines in the Market Place until the longer days, to minimise interference with business. The contractors are hopeful that the work will be completed by May. The company will commence paying for electricity from May 1st 1905, whether or no the cars are running'.*

With regard to the tramcars they were described *'as of the Nottingham pattern with seats for 22 passengers inside and 36 on top. The enquiry of the Light Railway Commissioners as to the application for extensions to Skegby and Forest Town is expected at an early date'.* There were also plans for an extension from the Nottingham Road terminus to the Cemetery, but none of these extensions was ever built.

In its edition of 16 June 1905, the *Mansfield Advertiser* informed its readers that *'The inauguration of a tramcar service on the Mansfield and District Light Railways has at last reached a stage which suggests a fulfilment of the scheme. About 3am last Friday morning, officials gathered at the temporary car sheds on Chesterfield Road and after the current had been switched on, car No 1, passed smoothly out, after which a most satisfactory run was made to New England (Pleasley) the distance being covered in about 10 minutes. Meanwhile, rail laying continues in the Market Place, Stockwell Gate and West Gate'.*

Finally, in its edition of 14 July 1905, the paper was able to announce that on the afternoon of 11 July two representatives of the Board of Trade, Major Pringle and Mr A P Trotter, had visited Mansfield for the purpose of inspecting the first completed sections.

The sections inspected were from the Market Place to Nottingham Road (or Berry Hill Lane as it was known) and to the borough boundary at Pleasley. Two cars were provided, Nos.4 and 6, the latter for the official inspection party and the former for members of Mansfield Corporation. Starting at 2pm, a run was made from the railway viaduct in Albert Street to Berry Hill Lane, then back into town and out to Pleasley. Before allowing the Berry Hill Lane route to be opened to the public the officials ordered some further road widening in Albert Street where an ancient hostelry, the 'Old White Bear' had to be demolished to permit the necessary work. The rest of the system having been approved, the service to the public was commenced at 5pm that day when, in the presence of a large and enthusiastic crowd of onlookers, the Mayor of Mansfield, Mr G H Hibbert, accompanied by his lady wife, the deputy mayor Mr J E Alcock and other officials representing the tramcar manufacturers, the Corporation and the tramway company, boarded car No.4 outside the Town Hall. His Worship purchased the first ticket No.000, the deputy mayor purchased ticket No.001 and the mayoress, No.002.

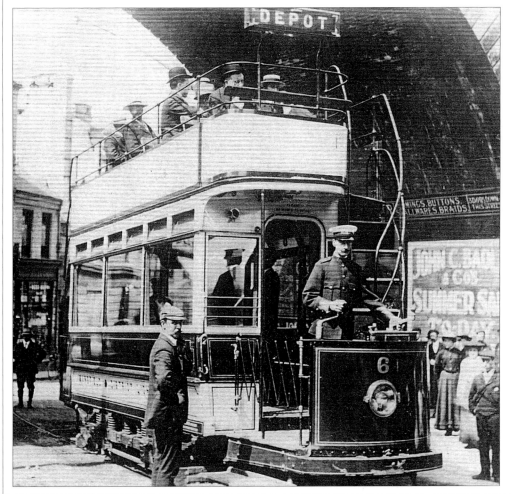

An interesting photograph of car No.6 carrying the official inspection party of Major Pringle and Mr A P Trotter. The car had left the Market Place at 2pm on Tuesday 11 July 1905 and shortly afterwards stopped in Albert Street beneath the arches of the Midland Railway viaduct which is when this photograph was taken. The inspectors registered dissatisfaction with the width of the road at this point and work had to be carried out before the service to Nottingham Road could commence. Photograph courtesy Mr R Cooke.

The first trams arrived in Mansfield by train from Scotland before the depot in Sutton Road was ready for them, so they were assembled in the roadway. Here is car No.4 being matched up with its wheels and truck with a crowd of interested onlookers in the background. Photograph courtesy Adam Gordon.

Open top Hurst, Nelson car No.3 stands at Nottingham Road (Berry Hill Lane) terminus. The crew are not in uniform so we may take it that this was a trial run prior to the Board of Trade inspection. Photograph courtesy Dr R G P Tebb.

The first tramcar on public service leaves the Market Place for Pleasley on 11 July 1905. The Mayor, Mr G H Hibbert, resplendent in ceremonial white top hat, is at the controls, with his lady wife at his side. The gent on the left, with hand on hip, is Mr Charles Robert Walker, the engineer and general manager of the company. Photograph Mansfield Museum.

Resplendent in his chain of office and wearing his official white top hat, the Mayor took the controls of the car. Scores of small boys were told to 'shift', a handle was moved and the car suddenly leapt forward at such a speed as to make the passengers who were standing reel. Children clapped, smiled and waved hands. Apparently, every house in Mansfield was forsaken for the pleasure of seeing the first car. Under the watchful eye of the official driver, the Mayor drove the car round into Westgate where he handed the controls back to the driver.

The next day (Wednesday 12 July 1905) the first full day's operation commenced when the first car left the

Five of the six new Brush covered top double deck trams appear in this photograph taken in Mansfield depot in 1906. Car No.13, which was the favourite, is probably off posing elsewhere. No.15 displays the destination 'Skegby Station'. This was on the proposed Skegby and Teversal line which never materialised. The other cars have the destination 'Hucknall under Huthwaite' although the 'Huthwaite' is actually under the 'Hucknall'! This was later shortened to Huthwaite. Photograph Mansfield Museum.

Market Place for Pleasley at 4.45am. The Berry Hill route followed soon after, the necessary works having been completed in Albert Street.

The Sutton route was inspected by the Board of Trade officials on 18 December 1905 and the line opened that day. The extension to 'Hucknall under Huthwaite', later known simply as 'Huthwaite' was officially opened in February 1906.

Meanwhile, work had still not commenced on the Mansfield Woodhouse route, and in connection with this a petition had been received by the company from the Leeming Street tradespeople, asking for the company to pave the tracks with wooden blocks instead of granite setts. Leeming Street being very narrow and busy, they feared that the noise would be intolerable. The company replied that they would gladly do this if the tradespeople would pay for the extra cost of wooden blocks, the difference in cost to be decided by the Borough Engineer.

Negotiations were taking place to make use of a new road (Yorke Street) into Mansfield Woodhouse, on the Duke of Portland's estate. A Mr Herbert Ashley of Mansfield had tendered for this work in the sum of £1,578 and this was agreed to, subject to the Duke's approval. Negotiations provided protracted for it was not until 26 November 1907 that the Mansfield Woodhouse section was finally completed.

For the first five years after opening, the trams served Mansfield Woodhouse, Sutton and Huthwaite, Pleasley and Berry Hill Lane (Nottingham Road). Extensions were proposed to Crown Farm to serve the newly opened Mansfield Colliery, also to Skegby, Rainworth, Forest Town and

Clipstone. It was noticeable that all the routes and proposed routes, apart from Berry Hill, served the collieries which were then opening to exploit the rich local coal seams.

On 23 February 1911 the *Mansfield Chronicle* was able to report that: '*the matter of the Crown Farm Extension had been most carefully considered by the Mansfield and District Tramways Board and they had come to the unanimous conclusion that the time had come to take in hand the extension. They were glad to state that they were able to make a vigorous start and barring accidents, they hoped that the line would be ready for public use in the course of a few months and possibly earlier, as it was believed that the contractors had made up their minds to build it in a very short time*'.

Made up their mind they had indeed, for on 20 April 1911, less than two months after the above report, the *Mansfield Chronicle* announced that the new tramway extension to Mansfield Colliery 'was officially inspected last Thursday afternoon on behalf of the Board of Trade by Major Pringle and shortly afterwards a service of cars commenced.'

The new service commenced in Church Street and not in the Market Place as the other routes did. Church Street was fairly narrow at the point where it was proposed that the trams would start and the Major was handed a petition on behalf of the traders and residents of Church Street, stating that 'they would be most injuriously affected' by the running of trams in Church Street. They objected to the service being authorised for various reasons, among them that Church Street was exceedingly narrow and the ordinary traffic there very heavy (in

1911!). It was particularly congested on Thursdays and Saturdays; moreover, traffic was likely to increase in the near future as the street was the main thoroughfare to Mansfield Colliery (which the tramway was designed to serve) and to the proposed new Great Central Mansfield railway station in Ratcliff Gate. In addition it was intended to erect a new Post Office in the street. In view of these facts the petitioners considered that it would be 'a source of danger and inconvenience to the public, to permit the Church Street to be used by the company.'

This somewhat 'NIMBY' attitude by the Church Street petitioners was given short shrift by the Major who said that it was far too late to present a petition of this type and that it ought to have been done when the initial enquiry was being held in the town. However, he did agree that it was a potentially dangerous location and he would do what he could to improve matters by 'appointing certain stopping places and regulating the pace of the cars'. Appointment and regulation having been carried out, the trams were soon up and running, as noted in the newspaper reports.

Having negotiated the dangers of Church Street, the tramcars then passed by the parish church of St Peter's and St Paul's, threading their way along Bridge Street before passing under the bridge adjacent to the station of the newly constructed Mansfield Railway line to Mansfield Colliery and Tuxford. The tramway then turned sharp left into Newgate Lane, ascended a sharp rise, then followed Newgate Lane for about a quarter of a mile before reaching the junction with Pecks Hill, where there was a loop in the line. This was at the foot of what was to become notorious Skerry Hill which, with a gradient of 1 in 10, was stated to be one of the steepest elevations in Mansfield. At the top of the hill was a crossroads with Carter Lane. The line then followed the Eakring Road as far as the cross roads with Oak Tree Lane, a very rural location in those days, but situated adjacent to the Mansfield Colliery. This was the Crown Farm terminus. The total cost of the extension was £17,200.

Top. Car No.3 at the Nottingham Road terminus on a trial run. The passengers are probably representatives of the Tramway Company and Mansfield Corporation.
Photograph Mansfield Museum.

Hurst Nelson cars Nos.7, 3 and 6 and Brush car No.14 in the Sutton Road depot, about 1910. Photograph Mansfield Museum.

The two railway overbridges on Nottingham Road. The nearer bridge carried the Mansfield Railway and at 16ft 3ins was the lowest overbridge on the system, too low for some cars to pass under. Photograph courtesy B Lund, Recollections of a Bygone Age.

Mr Charles Robert Walker, resident engineer during the construction of the tramway and later General Manager and secretary. Photograph courtesy Old Mansfield Society.

Chapter 5
The 1906 Tramway Strike

The strike which took place on the Mansfield and District Light Railways in 1906 has become part of the folklore of Mansfield and it is worth recording in some detail as an interesting insight into the social conditions in the town nearly 100 years ago. The tramway had been open barely one year and for some time there had been agitation for the employees to be allowed to join a Trades Union. Those responsible for making the demands had been told by the management to 'give up their unionism' or be dismissed.

There had evidently been some dissatisfaction amongst the employees over conditions of service and the posting of a new duty roster by the manager in September 1906 precipitated matters. The effect of the new roster was to reduce the hours worked and hence the pay. To compensate for this the men put in a claim for a small increase, to 6d per hour for drivers and 5d per hour for conductors. This the manager, Mr R C Walker declined and as a result all the men except one, a total of forty drivers and conductors, put in their notice.

This was at once accepted by the manager, who then immediately set about recruiting new staff in their place. Meanwhile, the men asked for a meeting to discuss the situation, to take place at the depot at midnight, this being the only time when all the staff were available. This was the usual time that staff meetings were held, and in fact the manager himself had previously called meetings at that hour. However, on this occasion he declined to attend complaining of the unreasonableness of the hour.

He then issued a statement on behalf of the company, which was quoted in the local newspaper. In it he said that as far as he was concerned there was no strike as such. Forty men had given in their notice and these had been accepted by the company. He was now recruiting new staff to take their place. There had been no discussions and he was prepared to show the men's pay rolls to show that what they were saying about the poor pay was incorrect. The newspaper report goes on to say that Mr Walker then gave the names of the motor men and conductors with their wages 'which appears below' – unfortunately this very interesting piece of information is missing. Mr Walker finished by announcing that services would continue 'as before' with the new men that he had engaged and that the company did not consider this to be in the way of a strike at all.

In answer to this a leaflet was hastily prepared by the men and handed out to the public. This read as follows: *'A protest against the Mansfield and District Light Railways Manager's Report in our weekly paper. (The Mansfield Chronicle). To the public of this district. We, the tramway employees contradict the manager's report as regards both wages and hours. We are only standing out for a living wage and our rights; live and let live. Yours faithfully, the Mansfield and District Light Railway Employees'.*

This simple statement stirred an outburst of public sympathy for the men, and a large crowd gathered in the Market Place to demonstrate where their sympathies lay. The level of public support for the men was described as 'remarkable'. Colliery workers announced that they were hiring horse drawn 'paddys' to take them to work and the Mansfield Football Club issued a statement that for their forthcoming away match with Sutton Town they would be travelling by 'brakes' instead of by tram, out of sympathy with the men on strike. On the following day only a few trams ran, there being of course insufficient trained staff to operate them and the manager himself was reported to be at the controls of a Pleasley car. The public had gathered in large numbers at various points along the line and the new drivers were subject to a torrent of abuse and some missiles, including eggs were thrown. Two men were arrested and dealt with at the

A view of Mansfield Market Place shortly after the opening in 1905 showing car No.3 in Market Street. Note that the track has not yet been extended into Leeming Street. Photograph Mansfield Museum.

Borough Sessions on the following Tuesday.

The men who had tendered their resignation had been told to hand in their uniforms immediately, but none had done so. A meeting was called at the Dial Hotel next to the Town Hall, and while the men were attending this meeting, another meeting was being held in the Market Place outside, to rally public support. A large and enthusiastic crowd had gathered to hear Alderman Pendleton, JP, speak on behalf of the men.

Some interesting facts emerge from this worthy gentleman's oration. Mr Walker, the manager, had said in his published statement that the average wage of drivers was 28 shillings per week and that of conductors, 24 shillings. Councillor Pendleton had in his possession two or three wage tickets. These showed that a regular conductor had in the last week drawn the magnificent sum of 16 shillings 0½d. From this there were deductions of 1 shilling 9½d plus sixpence club money. A driver's ticket showed a wage of 19 shillings 4d with 6d stoppages for a friendly society. This, said Councillor Pendleton, was Mr Walker's 28 shillings and 24 shillings. He said he would leave it to the public to decide whether any man could maintain a family with any standard of decency on a wage like that.

He then went into the Dial Hotel to address the men, on the question of 'ways and means'. He reminded them that a branch of the Tramway Workers Union had been formed and that some financial support would be given through the Trades Council. He also thought that the public would be making a subscription. He finished by advising the men to keep clear of any disturbance or violence.

Meanwhile, it was reported that the Mayor of Mansfield, Councillor J P Singleton, was not unmindful of what was taking place and during the course of that week had arranged several discussions with the Tramways Manager, Mr Walker, over the somewhat uncompromising attitude taken by the company. With the public firmly on the side of the strikers, the Mayor succeeded in arranging a meeting between representatives of the company and the workmen, in the hope that the atmosphere might be cleared somewhat.

The Mayor was supported by the Chairman of the Electricity Committee, Councillor Collins, who obviously stood to lose considerable business if the strike continued. Mr Walker was supported by Mr Balfour (later of Balfour, Beatty and Co) representing the company.

After the discussions, agreement was finally reached, with the company agreeing to a small increase in wages and the men agreeing to a small reduction in numbers, fewer staff being, in any case, required during the winter months. After this successful outcome, the Mayor addressed the waiting public from the steps of the Town Hall. It had been, he said 'a hard task', but he was glad that the issue was most satisfactorily resolved. He was sorry that there had been some criticism of Alderman Chadburn (the local director of the company) and he hoped that it would be a very long time before there was a similar dispute in the town. Alderman Pendleton then asked the public to record their appreciation of the efforts of Councillor Singleton and Collins in bringing about a settlement. Three cheers were raised for His Worship. The Mayor responded by thanking the Superintendent of Police for the tactful way they had dealt with the strike. Three cheers were then raised for the Police.

The men then returned to work. The first car, to Sutton and Huthwaite, contained His Worship the Mayor, together with Councillor Collins, Councillor Pendleton, a Mr Murdoch representing the company and other officials. The car made a triumphal entry into Sutton and Huthwaite. Thousands of people were reported as lining the route and 'cheering again and again'. Flags were displayed and there were many other signs of satisfaction on the part of the public at the settlement of the dispute.

So the strike came to an end and it is remarkable today, looking back, that despite the serious nature of the dispute, the sensible, even sensitive, handling of the affair by the Mayor and his team brought the whole thing to a speedy conclusion, with concessions on both sides, to the general satisfaction of all. Of such things are industrial relationship dreams made of! Attitudes were of course to be hardened by the 1926 General Strike and the Depression of the 1930s.

In it's Editorial Comment of 15 March 1907 the *Mansfield Chronicle* reported: *'The Light Railways, as a definite policy, do not allow the workmen to join a Trades Union. This may be a mistake. Had the men been so organised they would have had the advice of men experienced in these matters. The company would have been approached before extreme measures were taken and in all probability a strike would not have come about. Trade Unions are not always models of wisdom and moderation but they frequently confer great benefits for the employers as well as the employed, and there is much reason for believing that some good would have resulted in this case. To avoid the bitterness and passions engendered by strikes is always worth striving for'.*

Mr C R Walker has sometimes been cast as the villain of the piece, but as general manager he would have been expected to carry out the instructions of the company, whose head office was in London. Mr Chadburn was the local representative on the board of directors and as far as most Mansfield people were concerned Mr Chadburn was 'the company'. No doubt therein lies the source of the criticism levelled against him during the strike, referred to by the Mayor.

Names of employees included in the Manager's report on the 1906 strike have now come to light. They are:

Motormen: Lamin, Neville, Truman, Fryer, Skidmore, Wootton, Beckett, Richardson, Wright, Cooling, Malt, Parkes, Tatham (Charles Tatham, later acting manager), Underwood (Charles Underwood, later Chief Inspector), Williams, Starham, Morland (William Vane Morland, later manager Leeds City Tramways!) and Carter.

Conductors: Chapman, Gilbert, Bowne, Mayman, Cain, Graves, A Hawkins, Dellar, Kitchen, Smith, Peet, Goddard (aged 18), Thompson, Jeremiah Hooks, Topman, C Smith, Spinks and H Smith.

Crowds gathered in Mansfield Market in September 1906, to demonstrate sympathy for the striking tramway crews. Photograph Mansfield Museum.

Chapter 6
The Runaway Tram and other incidents

A number of mishaps befell before the tramway during its working life and the best known of these is the Skerry Hill runaway. This was well documented at the time and is worth repeating in some detail. Shortly after the opening of the Crown Farm line, the *Mansfield Chronicle* enticed its readers with lurid headlines in its edition of 25 January 1912. 'Runaway Tram' cried the headlines. 'Mansfield Miners' Thrilling Experience'. 'Several Men Injured, Graphic Description by Passengers'. So ran the journalistic sensationalism of the day, I can do no better than repeat the Chronicles' account of events which, in the language of those days, vividly recalls more of the folk lore of the town's tramways.

'A short while ago', the newspaper recalls, *'the Mansfield and District Tramway Co opened a new branch line from the Market Place to Forest Town and Mansfield Colliery and the cars had to traverse this particular] hill because it was on the direct route'*. This 'particular hill' was actually Skerry Hill and in fact the line never did serve Forest Town, which was on the proposed route to Clipstone Colliery, never built. Nevertheless let us continue our account:

'On the morning to question' runs the report (it does not actually say which morning it was) *'a tramcar filled with*

workmen employed at the Mansfield colliery started as usual from the Market Place at 6.15am and all went well until the car had nearly reached the top of Skerry Hill when, it is stated, the power went off, the lights went out and the car started to run backwards down the hill. No sooner was this noticed then there was a panic amongst the passengers. Some of the men jumped off and many were pushed off but happily no loss of life had to be recorded, although some of the workmen were more or less seriously injured and some sustained cuts and bruises but were however, after attention, able to proceed to their employment'.

Under the sub heading 'A General Panic' the newspaper account continues. There were three officials on the car – Charles Revill of Thoresby Street, Mansfield, an inspector employed by the Tramway Co, Arthur Pilkington of Bradder Street, the driver and J Overton of Mansfield Woodhouse, the conductor. The car was already heavily laden for when it reached the loop at foot of Skerry Hill, Inspector Revill requested the driver of a car returning empty from Crown Farm to turn back and help to convey some of the workmen to the colliery. The driver agreed and a number of passengers on the first car were persuaded by the Inspector to transfer

on to the second after it had run round the loop and was lined up ready to return to Crown Farm. A number of workmen who had been waiting at the stop also got on to the second car, so that it was soon full. The first car then set off up Skerry Hill with an estimated load of one hundred passengers! This was *after* some of them had been persuaded to take the second car. It was, according to reports, dark and foggy at the time so that the lights of the first car were soon lost to view.

After waiting for a few minutes, the driver of the second car started up the hill but about half way up he heard what sounded like a tram coming back down the hill towards him on the single track. Realising what had happened he threw open the saloon door and shouted a warning to the throng for some of them to get out. He then took his control handles to the other end of the car and began running back down the hill at a good speed. Some men jumped off as the first car could be seen and heard to be rapidly gaining ground. At the bottom of the hill both cars were brought to a halt by their drivers without damage or serious injury. Neither car became derailed nor even de-wired, a point commented on by the manager, Mr C R Walker, in his official report. In it he said that there were four early morning cars on which

Miners crowd on to a car at the recently opened Crown Farm terminus in 1911. No wonder the trams sometimes ran away down Skerry Hill! There are about 60 passengers on board and loads of a hundred were not uncommon when the miners were changing shifts at the nearby Mansfield Colliery. Photograph courtesy B Lund, Recollections of a Bygone Age.

Skerry Hill about 1911, shortly after the tramway was opened. It will be noted that the right-hand side of the roadway is as yet incomplete with a 'causey' (pavement) yet to be laid. One wonders if the gent on crutches was a victim of the runaway tram accident. Photograph courtesy Old Mansfield Society.

the miners crowded a great deal. This particular car had got to within ten yards of the top of the hill, when the fuse blew out and it began to run back. Mr Walker's report goes on to say, *'Some of the passengers got excited and, rushing to the driver's end, interfered with him! Luckily he stuck to the brakes and eventually pulled the car up ere it had reached the bottom of the hill'.*

The driver, Arthur Pilkington, received great praise from all parties for his calmness at a very trying time and quite rightly so. As if the tram running away were not enough without having his end interfered with by excited passengers, and miners at that! However the conductor, Mr Overton, was not so lucky as he was knocked off the front of the tram by the decamping passengers and his takings, amounting to 1s 8½d were 'squandered in all directions'. Inspector Charles Revill is reported to have shouted out 'It will be alright; stand still and keep your places.' This cut no ice with the miners and a mad panic to decamp had ensued. In his report, the manager said that if the men had kept their places, the car would have been checked sooner because the brakes were in perfect working order; at no time did the car get out of hand and the trolley pole never left the wire although the car was travelling backwards. There were no fatalities resulting although about

twenty men were unable to return to work that day.

There was some justified criticism of the company for the overloading of its cars. Despite their being an inspector on board, there were said to be men standing not only inside the car but on the steps, on both sets of stairs and the front and back platforms were also packed. This was clearly in contravention of Board of Trade Regulations although it has been stated that tramway officials were powerless to prevent overcrowding as the company was officially operating as a 'light railway'.

There are numerous reports of trams losing power and running back down Skerry Hill, also down Stockwell Gate Hill. Some of these accidents were due to chronic overloading which overcame the cars' ability to carry a 50 percent overload.

Other runaways were due to what would nowadays be called 'human error'. Such an incident occurred on Saturday 13 July 1906 about 7.30pm when a car which had been taken out of service with a reported faulty handbrake was being manoeuvred into the Sutton Road depot. This stood at the top of Stockwell Gate Hill, which had a gradient of 1 in 26. The car started to roll back down the hill towards the town. Driver William Shepperson tried to stop it but was unable to do so and jumped off.

Inspector Biddulph remained at the controls to try to control the runaway. The car ran down the hill, negotiated the Red Lion loop at the foot of the hill at some speed and then careered on down Stockwell Gate, a very narrow and busy thoroughfare on the single track. The driver of another car, in Stockwell Gate, saw the approaching runaway, applied the handbrake of his car lightly, then leapt off the platform. Inspector Biddulph leapt off the runaway and the two cars collided, fortunately without loss of life. Despite the serious nature of the smash, services were reported to be running normally within half an hour.

It is interesting to note that driver Shepperson's name does not appear in the list of drivers and conductors published shortly after this event, in connection with the tramway strike. It is to be hoped that Inspector Biddulph however, received some recognition for his brave conduct in remaining at the controls of the runaway car – a truly terrifying experience.

Another serious incident occurred on Stockwell Gate Hill nearly two years later, on Friday 17 April 1908. A car from Sutton, driven by Christopher George of Spencer Street, Mansfield, with conductor Harry Allaway also of Mansfield, stopped at the depot on Sutton Road. Two Inspectors, Michael O'Reilly and Walter Hopewell boarded the car on their way down to the

Market Place. The car then began to descend Stockwell Gate Hill and soon started to build up speed, to what has been described variously as between 10 and 30 miles per hour.

As the car approached the Red Lion loop at the foot of the hill, it was reported to be rocking and swaying. It was then that a girl was seen to fall from the rear platform of the car. The girl, Mary Ann Webster aged 18 years of Silverhill Cottages, Teversal, near Sutton, received injuries from which she subsequently died. At the resulting inquest into the accident the staff denied that the car had been travelling at excessive speed. The manager, Mr C R Walker, had had the car examined and it was in perfect working order.

It proved impossible to determine whether the girl had attempted to jump off the car whilst in motion or whether she had been thrown off as a result of the rocking and swaying induced by the allegedly excessive speed. The jury returned a verdict of accidental death with a recommendation that there should be a compulsory stopping place halfway down Stockwell Gate Hill.

As a result, the Board of Trade made a statutory order (No.533) dated 19 June 1908 stating that 'in addition to existing regulations, the carriages on the (light) railway, shall be brought into a standstill on Sutton Road (sic) immediately before passing Padley

Hill on the downward journey'. The number of accidents is not to be wondered at when the primitive braking methods are considered.

Another rather less dramatic incident is recalled by Mr Reg Cooke, son of Alf Cooke, one-time Mansfield tram driver. There was a tailor's shop in Westgate where MacDonalds now stands, who advertised himself in large letters over his shop as 'Stewart the King of Tailors' in the rather grandiose manner of those times. One day a passing tram became dewired and the trolley pole went straight through the middle of Mr Stewart's advert, smashing it in half. When the trolley pole was finally extricated the hoarding over the shop now exclaimed 'Stew ... the King ...!' This caused some raised eyebrows in the town and the offending hoarding was quickly removed!

An accident well remembered by Mansfield folk occurred when the supply from the electricity power station failed. Shortly after 5.15pm on Friday 1 September 1916 Harry Witts was driving a Mansfield Woodhouse bound car up Leeming Street when suddenly, about half way up, the power went off. He managed to coast his car back down the gradient and came to a halt at the bottom, much to the consternation of the policeman directing traffic at this point. However, the officer soon had more than this to contend with when, speeding

backwards down Stockwell Gate came a tram which had only minutes before departed for Sutton and Huthwaite. This was car No.1, driven by John C Harrison of 68 Carlton Street, Mansfield with lady conductor Phoebe Carrol of Victoria Terrace. The car was lightly laden and had left the Market Place at 5.15pm. The car stopped halfway up Stockwell Gate Hill to pick up passengers and when the driver attempted to get under way, there was no power and the car commenced to run back down the hill. A high speed was attained and witnesses described the tram as travelling 'like an express train'.

Some passengers managed to jump off and at the junction with Westgate, the car left the rails and embedded itself in the front of Carrs Shoe Shop in Market Chambers. The only casualty in this remarkable event was a lad named Sam Shawcroft who was knocked down and injured in the road. Fortunately he made a complete recovery.

Below. **Car No.20 stands at the Crown Farm terminus some time in the 1920s. The terminus at this time presented a completely rural aspect, being constructed mainly for the benefit of miners at the Mansfield Colliery. Note the sloping shield fitted over the bumper of No.20 to prevent unauthorised passengers standing on the bumper when the car was full. Photograph courtesy Mansfield Museum.**

Above. Brush built car No.17, travelling along Outram Street, Sutton, towards Mansfield, in the early days of the tramway. The footpaths are crowded with ladies, many wearing aprons and some fashionable hats. They may be just turned out from a local hosiery mill. In the background can be seen the local gasworks and outside the office is a very fine street light (gas of course). The photograph was taken about 1909 and one of the changes soon to be brought about by the Great War was in ladies' fashions. Photographs taken immediately after the war show that full length skirts, starched aprons and fine hats had almost vanished from the scene. Photograph courtesy Sutton Library.

Left. Tram No.1 after its involvement in a serious smash. It is likely that this was as a result of the car running away down Stockwell Gate Hill and coming off the track at the junction of Westgate, before colliding with the front of Carrs Shoe shop in Market Chambers. The gent contemplating events is a Mr Wharmby. Date about 1916. Photograph courtesy B Lund, Recollections of a Bygone Age.

Chapter 7
More Tramcars

In 1911, the extension to Crown Farm was opened. This, and the hopeful prospect of further extensions, prompted the company to place orders for several more cars. It is generally accepted that the order for the bulk of these went to the United Electric Car Co of Preston. Unfortunately, the written records which survive are very incomplete and several unsolved mysteries remain. What is known is that the UEC Co delivered two new cars later in 1911. These were four wheeled closed top double deckers, with open balconies and vestibules. They were numbered 21 and 22 in the Mansfield fleet and were fitted with GE K10D controllers Peckham P22 trucks and two BTH GE67 40hp motors. They were thus a big improvement over the earlier cars with their 25hp motors.

The new cars had four windows to each side of the saloons and full length roof tops, unlike the earlier Brush cars which had unusually short roof covers over the balconies. They retained, however, the wooden longitudinal close lath seating in the lower saloon and the garden seat arrangement on the top deck. Seating was provided for 56 passengers, although the Board of Trade returns group them in the 61-80 seats category. In 1912, the company took delivery of two more cars, but these were completely different to 21 and 22. It is not even certain that they came from UEC, but it is more than likely that they did so, although from photographs they were in appearance

more like the original Hurst Nelson cars, with open vestibules, quarter turn stairs and a short canopy over the vestibule. Why Mansfield went back to this type of car is a mystery. It may be that they were obtained cheaply being of a rather antiquated design or it may be that the company, being extremely satisfied with the original simple Hurst Nelson cars, wanted something similar instead of the big, heavy and expensive to operate covered top cars. Whatever the reason, these two cars were numbered 23 and 24 in the Mansfield fleet. A further mystery then follows. The Board of Trade returns for 1913 show a further car being delivered to Mansfield. Nothing is known about this car at all, unless it refers to the works/snowplough car discussed in 1905.

The author, however, is inclined to doubt the existence of this mysterious 1913 car. It is unlikely that the works car would have been included in the Board of Trade returns. The Board of Trade returns were of course accurate only insofar as the information fed to them by the company was accurate, rather like the information gleaned from computers in this modern age. The company may have been anticipating the delivery of a new car which never arrived. The UEC company were flat out providing cars amongst others for the recently opened Notts and Derby tramway, with which the Mansfield company were associated and Mansfield may have agreed to a delay in a delivery date until the following

year. This is all speculation, but from the available evidence it appears unlikely that this odd car ever actually arrived in Mansfield. The following year, 1914, of course, saw the outbreak of the Great War and production of trams for the home market ground to a halt as factories shifted to production of munitions and weapons of war. By Ministry of Munitions decree, orders for new trams would have to be vetted by themselves and only in extreme cases would permission be given.

Despite this, in July 1916 the directors of the Mansfield company reported the need for extra cars. An application was made to the Ministry and the coveted Certificate A was obtained enabling the company to place an order with the United Electric Car Co at Preston for four covered top open balcony cars, at a cost of £1,080 each. What persuaded the Minister to grant a Certificate to Mansfield it is impossible to say. Perhaps it was something to do with maintaining output from the pits, extra cars being needed to transport the colliers. These cars were similar to the ones delivered in 1911 and to those delivered to the Notts and Derby company.

It is interesting to note that during this period only Mansfield, the South Lancashire Tramways and Sunderland Corporation were successful in obtaining permission for new cars, in the latter case to replace one destroyed in a Zeppelin raid. By the end of the war Mansfield had 28 trams but two were soon disposed of. These went to

Car no 22 bound for Huthwaite, loads in Portland Square, Sutton about 1916. Photograph courtesy Sutton library.

the Llanelly and District Electric Lighting and Traction Co who in their minutes of 11 June 1918 noted the purchase of two cars from the Mansfield and District Tramways for the sum of £520 each; minutes of 12 December 1918 record that the sum of £1042.19.7d had been paid to Mansfield for the purchase of two cars.

In the minutes of the Mansfield and District Light Railway Co, dated 28 October 1918, the sale of two cars to the Llanelly Company for the sum of £1,020 was noted. These were the two open top cars Nos.23 and 24, which it is believed became Llanelly Nos.13 and 14.

The six UEC cars remaining in Mansfield took the numbers 21 to 26, number 21 and 22 being the 1911 cars and 23 to 26 the four 'wartime' cars. We may assume that the latter were in every way similar to those delivered to the associated Notts and Derby Tramway Company at nearby Langley Mill, which was another member of the Balfour Beatty group. These cars were 27ft 6 inches long, 15ft 6 inches high, headroom in lower saloon was 6ft 4inches and in the upper saloon, 6ft

Above. **Open top car No.24 passing the old cattle market on Nottingham Road. The origin of this car and its sister No.23 are uncertain but it is believed that they were both sold to Llanelly in 1918 shortly after this photograph was taken and their numbers taken by two of the cars ordered from the UEC in 1916. Photograph courtesy D Ottewell.**

0inches. Unladen weight was 13 tons 10cwt. The cars were mounted on Peckham P22 trucks. This appears to be the position as far as can be determined with regard to the UEC cars. There have been other interpretations, but without the benefit of records and orders, the position may never be fully clarified. The author would welcome further information with regard to these rather sketchy details.

Market Street, Mansfield looking up to the Midland Railway viaduct just prior to World War I. The car is open top No.23 which with its sister car No.24 presents something of a mystery as to its origin. Note that No.23 is moving off on the right-hand track towards Nottingham Road, while the overhead trolley is on the left-hand wire. The trams usually ran into the Market Place from Nottingham Road on the nearside of the loop line, then returned on the same line, the trolley meanwhile having been reversed. This caused endless problems in later years when motor traffic became so prevalent. In this photograph the only vehicle affected is a horse and cart which is in any case proceeding along the wrong side of the road! Photograph courtesy OMS.

Chapter 8
Cow on the Line and other incidents

The Mansfield tramway system was no more accident prone than any other but nevertheless had its fair share of incidents. A remarkable accident occurred on Christmas Eve 1925 when a car was entering the loop at the Old Blue Bell, on Alfreton Road, Sutton. As it did so the sprung point blade left the bed of the track, shot up and pierced the floor of the car. As a result a Mrs Speed of Sutton received two broken legs and a Miss Kersey of Huthwaite was badly bruised. Mr R F Dixon, the manager, said that the accident was caused by a build up of ice and snow in the points. No doubt a civil claim resulted from the accident, as it had done 10 years previously, when a local farmer had sued the Light Railway company for £24.17.3d as a result of his cow having been knocked down and killed by a tram.

The circumstances of this case were almost comical with shades of both George Stephenson and the Reverend Awdry's Thomas the Tank Engine. The farmer, John Gilbert Wright of Huthwaite, had bought what was described as a prize cow at a local auction on Wednesday 15 January 1916. About 6.15pm the farmer's son was driving the cow home along the road from Sutton to Huthwaite when he saw a tram approaching along the single track near Sutton cemetery. He tried to warn the driver by whistling and shouting but the tram dashed into the beast and killed it. The tram was allegedly travelling at a fast speed and ran on 'fully a dozen yards' before it could be stopped. The plaintiff contended that the cow had as much right to be on the road as the tram and the tram driver was guilty of gross negligence.

Under cross examination the farmer's son admitted that it was dark at the time and the cow was walking on the track. He thought it would be alright as there were no trams coming, although there was plenty of room for the animal on either side of the track. When he saw the tram approaching he tried to get the cow off the line by using a stick he was carrying but he could not. He tried to attract the driver's attention but was unable to do so and an accident resulted.

Mr Young, representing the plaintiff: *'Are you aware of any rules for driving cattle on the road?'*

Witness. *'I suppose there are some'.*

Mr Young. *'You should have told the cow so!' (laughter)*

Judge. *'There are no rules for cattle. They go where they like.'*

Mr Young. *'The Mansfield trams also break the rules of the road. They wobble about all over the place!' (laughter).*

James William Crowder of Brownlow Road was the driver of the tram. He said that it was dark at the time and he did not see the cow until just before he hit it. He said that he did not hear any whistling or shouting although several passengers on the car gave evidence that they did.

Mr Young. *'How old are you?'* – '18 years'.

'You are very young to be a licensed motor man'.

Judge (interrupting) *'When I was 18 I thought I could do anything'.*

Mr Young. *'It is hardly fair to expect you to use the same discretion and judgement at 18 as a man would.'*

Mr White, representing the tramway company. *'You should blame the government for taking all the men.'*

Mr Young. *'What do you blame for not seeing the cow?'*

Driver. *'Well it was the same colour as the night –black!'*

Open top car No.5 at Sutton Cemetery, near to the site of the collision with a cow, which resulted in a court action against the tramway company. Photograph courtesy Sutton Library.

Skerry Hill, Mansfield in the 1920s. The baby Austin car, apparently under full throttle, attempts an ascent of Pecks Hill which runs off to the left of St. Laurence's Church and which would have been the road followed by the proposed tramway extension to Forest Town and Clipstone. The man with the "cleaning up" shovel is leading his horse and cart across the tram loop at the foot of the Skerry Hill. Photograph courtesy Mansfield Museum.

The conductor then gave evidence, giving his name as Sidney Guilor of Belmont Terrace, Mansfield. He said he was on the top deck collecting fares and heard no shouts or whistling.

Mr Young. 'And how old might you be, Mr Conductor?' – 'Fifteen years, sir'.

'I suppose you were too busy with your duties at the time. Even in Sutton you have to be careful they do not give you too much change.'

'It's not that sir, you have to be careful about French coins. Passengers do try it on sometimes.' (laughter).

Cissie Dickens of Huthwaite was another passenger who heard no shouts or whistles. She was obviously an attractive young lady as the questioning went as follows:

Mr Young. 'Were you alone at this time?' – 'Yes'

Mr Young. 'Surely you were talking to someone?' – 'No'.

'And did the other folks let you sit there without speaking to you?' – 'Yes.'

'You sat alone?' – 'Yes'

'Doing what?' – 'Nothing'.

Mr White. 'Probably thinking happy thoughts!'

Mr Young. 'About your bottom drawer perhaps.' (laughter).

Mr Young. 'Were you thrown into anyone's lap as a result of the crash?' – 'No'.

'No such luck then' (laughter).

Mr White, representing the company, said that the case against the company had not been made out:

'The car was being driven properly in a place where it had every right to be and was properly lighted. The company were not trying to say that the plaintiff should have a light on the cow' (laughter).

Judge. 'If he did not have a light he is guilty of contributory negligence. If he did he is a German spy!' (laughter).

Finally the judge, summing up, said that the points to be considered were whether Mr Wright shouted and whether the tram driver was taking sufficient precautions. The weight of evidence tended to show that Wright did shout out and whilst appreciating the difficulties faced by the driver, the claim against the company would be allowed.

A more sombre incident occurred on Saturday 27 May 1916 in Chatsworth Road, when a 2 year old child, Walter Moseley ran across the road and was knocked down by a tram and killed.

The driver, Mr W T Ward said that he applied both magnetic and hand brake hard; the car was travelling at 6mph and pulled up within 28 feet, the minimum braking distance at this speed.

Unfortunately the lifeguard failed to activate and the acting manager of the tramway, Mr J Ackland, said that when the gate and lifeguard were examined they were found to be in good working order. He said there had never been a problem previously and both children and dogs had been picked up on the lifeguard in the past. Mr Ackland expressed sympathy for the family, the father being a private soldier on active service with the Sherwood Foresters. The coroner returned a verdict of 'Accidental death' with no blame attached to the driver who did everything humanly possible.

A rather less serious accident occurred on Saturday 26 August 1916 at Sutton, when two cars were passing at a loop. The trolley rope of one car caught a passenger on the other and dragged him off the top deck. He fell heavily on the ground but was reported as 'not being seriously injured'!

Chapter 9
Post War Plans 1919-1926

Plans were deposited in March 1919 showing proposed tramway extensions to Forest Town, Clipstone Colliery and Rainworth, and a public enquiry was held by the Light Railway Commissioners, Captain Henry Alan Steward and Mr Alan D Erskine in May of that year, at Mansfield Town Hall. The plans were generally supported by the local councils, including Mansfield Corporation. However, Mr J D Fidler representing Sutton in Ashfield Urban District Council said that he was disappointed that the company were applying for further extensions when they had not built the lines approved 12 years ago, namely, to Skegby and Teversal.

The deposited plans showed the Rainworth line following the Southwell Road, with the line to Forest Town and Clipstone branching off along Carter Lane and not as an extension of the Crown Farm route as originally proposed. Objection to the proposals came from the Mansfield Railway Company, part of the Great Central Railway, one of whose directors was Mr William Jackson Chadburn. Their objection was on the grounds that they already had a line to Clipstone and although this was disused at present they might wish to recommence the service if the proposed housing developments took place in the district. (They never did of course and the line was lifted soon after).

The Light Railway Commissioners granted the application on certain conditions and the *Mansfield Advertiser* of Friday May 23 1919 announced 'Trams to Forest Town and Rainworth'. The article went on to say that the Light Railway Commissioners had approved the application for extensions, subject to the following conditions:

1. The Clipstone line be restricted in length so as not to compete unduly with the Mansfield Railway Co's line.

2. No goods to be carried on the tramway in excess of 56lb.

3. The application to increase fares on the existing routes was also approved to 1½p per mile.

4. The company to pay for the removal and resiting of posts, brackets etc in case of road widening being carried out by Mansfield Corporation.

5. The tracks to be paved with granite setts and Mansfield Corporation to be paid for tarmacadam where necessary.

6. The company were also required to pay half the cost of improvements to the corner of Carter Lane and Skerry Hill.

Mansfield Corporation were also granted the right to purchase the line outright after 30 years, including those sections in Mansfield Woodhouse and Southwell District Council, if those local authorities did not wish to

A smartly turned out car at the Sutton Road depot. In front of the car stands the manager Mr R F Dixon in the raincoat and behind him, Joe Tranter, the works supervisor. Between them, these two gents were reputed to run the tramways. The day is Good Friday 1922, and car No.11 was the first Hurst, Nelson car to be rebuilt from its original open top condition. Several others were also rebuilt but it was a leisurely programme and rebuilt cars were turned out only once every six months. At that rate it would have taken fifteen years to rebuild the whole fleet. Photograph National Tramway Museum.

Car No.25 stands in Mansfield Market Place in 1925, waiting to move off up Stockwell Gate to Sutton and Huthwaite. An interesting selection of motor vehicles is to be seen on the opposite side of the road; beyond can be seen Market Chambers and Carrs Shoe Shop, rammed by runaway car No.1 in 1916. Photograph courtesy Old Mansfield Society.

purchase it. Having successfully obtained their order, the company now set about raising the capital to finance the proposed extensions which would have increased the length of lines operated by about five miles.

	1914	1918
Rails	£6 per ton	£17.10s per ton
Setts	18s	26s
Cement	34s	129s
Trolley Wire	£102/mile	£189/mile
Span wire	16s 6d/cwt	48s/cwt
Gear wheels	£3.2s each	£13.18s each
Pinions	10s each	£2.15s.6d each
Tyres	28s each	£4.8.6d each
Armature coils	£5 per set	£17.5s per set
Trolley Heads	26s 3d each	£2.16s.3d each
Oil	1s/gallon	3s/gallon
Tickets	3d/1000	1s 3d/1000

Unfortunately, 1920 proved an exceptionally difficult year and the increasingly heavy costs of material and labour rendered the works financially impossible.

Wages had increased and the company were also worried about the freedom granted to the Mansfield Railway to restart their service to Clipstone; so much so that they later applied to have the proviso revoked.

There was little chance of the railway reintroducing this service but it continued to be a bogey man to the tramway company.

The following figures, for which I am greatly indebted to Edgar Jordan of Reading, shows the difference in prices paid for typical items of tramway equipment before and after the Great War..

In the minutes of the company's board meeting, held on 31 January 1919, the death of Mr Charles Robert Walker was noted with regret. The former general manager of the tramway, Mr Walker had left Mansfield in 1916 to take up a similar position with the newly opened Notts and Derby Tramway Company, another Balfour Beatty enterprise, but had remained in contact with his old company, as Secretary. Mr Chadburn had set up a trust for Mr Walker's daughter and the directors placed on record their sincere regret at the loss of a loyal colleague and friend. They also placed on record

their appreciation of the services rendered by Mr Chadburn during Mr Walker's last illness and in particular his visits to Mr Walker at Torquay during the last days of his life. Mr Walker had been suffering from the influenza which had affected a great many people in the years immediately after the First World War, and died at the comparatively young age of 48.

Mr Stanley Dudman was acting manager, but there is no doubt that the company sorely missed Mr Walker's expert guidance at this critical time. Mr Dudman was assisted by Mr J Ackland who was also assistant manager of the Notts and Derby tramway, so the association between the two companies was very close. The new manager of the Notts and Derby system it is worth noting, was none other than William Vane Morland, by now Captain Morland, who had started his career as a lad in the tramsheds at Mansfield.

An agreement was reached with Balfour Beatty and Co to double the track on Sutton Road and place it on sleeper track at the roadside at a cost of £25,000. An extension to the bus depot on Sutton Road was also approved.

In 1920 a new manager took up his post at Mansfield. Mr J R Dixon had had previous experience at Hull and Southampton, both very 'tram minded' cities, and a number of improvements took place under his guidance.

Rebuilding of the Hurst Nelson cars commenced, with top covers added to Nos.1, 4, 9 and 11. Car No.11 was the first to be rebuilt and was completed on Good Friday 1922. Thereafter the rebuilds were completed at the rate of one every six months. Brush car No.17 was rebuilt with a full length roof, and Peckham P22 trucks were fitted to most cars. The Westinghouse 90 controllers were largely replaced by Westinghouse T2A or BTH B18 controllers.

Various improvements were carried out to the track layout. Track was laid to the side of the road to facilitate loading at Pleasley and Huthwaite termini and the 2 mile section of reserved track at the side of Sutton Road was completed, replacing the single line down the middle of the road past Kings Mill reservoir. A short paved section of reserved track was laid at Bull Farm on the Pleasley Route, and additional passing loops were provided. It is also believed that the loops in Mansfield Market were extended about this time.

On 9 May 1922, Mr William Jackson Chadburn died at Mansfield. He had been one of the founder directors of the company and a champion of the tramways. His passing marked the start of a gradual change of heart in the local authorities' attitude towards the trams and things never seemed the same again.

By February 1925 the company felt in better shape financially and made a further application for extension of routes to Clipstone Colliery village, Rufford Colliery, Rainworth and Blidworth (colliery). Some of these proposals included placing the tramway on reserved track at the side of the road and in the case of the Clipstone extension, they were to be laid on the trackbed of the old Clipstone Camp railway line which had formerly run alongside the Clipstone Road. The line along Carter Lane had been replaced by one running off the Crown Farm route up Pecks Hill; there was also a proposal to extend the line from the Rainworth terminus alongside the private road to Rufford Colliery.

The application was heard on 2 February before the two commissioners representing the Ministry of Transport, Mr Alan D Erskine and Mr Thomas D Patterson. A room had been booked for the enquiry at Mansfield Town Hall; however, such was the number of representatives attending that a larger room at the adjacent County Court building had to be taken.

Mr Craig Henderson opened the case for the tramway company. He drew attention to the increase in the population of the district served by the tramway since it was inaugurated, which was in the region of 90 percent. He recalled the difficulties experienced by the company since the last application in 1919, particularly with regard to the objections raised by the Mansfield Railway Company and the resultant restrictions put on the tramway to overcome those objections. He also reminded the enquiry of the extraordinary trade difficulties applying in 1920, when the heavy cost of labour and materials had rendered the works financially impossible at that time.

However, there were now new colliery proposals for Clipstone, Blidworth and Rufford and the colliery company intended to build new model villages for their workforce. These new developments had made it necessary for the tramway to apply for further powers instead of just asking for an extension of time for the original proposals, approved in 1919.

This speech, of which the above is a much condensed version, is nevertheless of great interest as it indicates that even at this late date the tramway was seeking to considerably extend the system. However, a major player in the stakes had changed sides. Mansfield Corporation was no longer supporting the tramway company's application. Mr Chadburn and his associates had

An unknown covered top car makes its way along Stockwell Gate towards Sutton Road, in the mid-1920s. The van on the left is just turning into Queen Street. Photograph courtesy Mansfield Museum.

Car No.26 loads in the Market place for Mansfield Woodhouse, in 1925. A carelessly parked Armstrong motor car obstructs the lorry which is obliged to wait until one or other moves off. The trams got the blame for this type of hold up whereas we now know that the motor car was the culprit! Photograph courtesy Old Mansfield Society.

long since passed on and a new breed of men had taken over, men who were dissatisfied with the old way of doing things and wanted to put Mansfield on the map as a modern, progressive industrial town. The councillors had motor cars and wanted somewhere to drive them without being delayed by noisy, slow old fashioned tram cars. The council intended to build a new 100 foot wide motor road along the Southwell Road, whatever the tramway company wanted. It was declared that all roads where the tram lines were laid should be widened to a minimum of 52 feet, at the tramway company's expense of course, to accommodate all the new motor cars and buses which were flooding onto the roads. The Mayor of Mansfield, Councillor J A Beck, a fearsome critic of the tramway system, gave evidence to the commission that the Corporation were thinking of providing their own service of motor buses. (This was the only time this proposal was ever heard of).

Mr Henderson (representing the tramway company) *'And do you think your buses would be delayed by the tramcars?'*

The Mayor. *'No, because the buses would always be in front!' (laughter).*

The Mansfield Corporation also objected to the proposals to run the tramlines at the side of the road on the verge as this would cause great difficulty if development were to take place at the side of the road or the road were to be widened. The newly opened section of roadside running along Sutton Road was given as an example of the difficulties caused by this type of construction.

His Grace the Duke of Portland was quoted as being in support of the proposals but only if the trams were to run down the centre of the roadway. His Grace, who was a prominent and influential personality in the affairs of the town, also felt that the period of five years requested by the company for the completion of the works was too long and that a completion date within two years should be set.

No doubt he and many others in the town were getting tired of the company failing to carry out the work when approved and then pleading that they needed more time. The Local Authority had told the tramway company to 'Get

on with it – or get out!' The LNER as successors to the Mansfield Railway continued their objection to the proposals even though there was no longer a railway at Clipstone camp. Their argument was that they might at some future date wish to restore the station if the population of the area continued to grow.

The chairman pointed out that they had used the same argument previously when there was at least a station at Clipstone. Now that the station had gone, there was no longer the same strength in the argument.

Mr Lees, representing the LNER, concurred and withdrew the objection. The chairman of the directors of the tramway company said that provided that the objections could be overcome and there were no more strikes they intended to make a 'vigorous commencement' and complete the works in about 18 months. He said that there was sufficient money to carry out the works and that it was intended to order ten new tramcars. The meeting then closed.

On Friday May 8 1925, an article appeared in the *Mansfield Reporter*: *'The Light Railway Commissioners have*

granted the Mansfield Tramway Company the necessary powers to carry out the extensions. They have decided that there should be a road width of 9ft 6ins on either side of the tracks. This will involve a great deal of road widening (presumably at the tramway co's expense). The commissioners also repealed the protection afforded to the railway company at the previous enquiry'.

Despite this victory and the assertion that a vigorous commencement would be made, *The Reporter* noted in its issue of 1 January 1926 (nearly nine months later) that no visible moves had been made. Three months after this, the General Strike commenced and all industry stopped work. The tramways stayed out until Saturday 15 May although a skeleton service of buses had run, manned by volunteers and with a police escort. Whey they returned to work, it was at the same rate of pay as before. The coal miners stayed out on strike and the *Mansfield Reporter* noted that *'the unsettled state of the industrial world was revealed in the half yearly report of the Mansfield Tramways Company. The prolonged coal strike together with severe motor bus competitions has made it necessary to conserve the financial resources of the company and no dividends will be paid.'*

This was really the end of any hopes that the company might have had for extending the tramway. The main priority was now to stay in business and Sir Joseph Niall was appointed chairman of the company in July 1926. Although by no means anti-tram, Sir Joseph was astute enough to realise that if the company were to have any future, it did not lay along tram lines.

Top. Car No.17 trundles along Outram Street, Sutton in Ashfield, on its way back to Mansfield about 1928. Photograph courtesy Mansfield Museum.

Right. Car no.28 loading passengers in Mansfield Market Place about 1930 before departing for Mansfield Woodhouse. None of the Mansfield trams were fitted with "vestibules" (windscreens) for the drivers.

Car No.9 stands in Mansfield Market Place in the early 1930s. This was one of the original open top cars fitted with a top cover in the 1920s. Photograph M J O'Connor, National Tramway Museum.

Chapter 10
On the Trams

The main source of information about the day to day working of the tramway has been the transcript of a tape recording made in 1983 of the memories of Eric Arthur Evans, one-time Mansfield tram driver and aged 74 at the time of the recording. We are extremely lucky to have this account and I for one would like to place on record my thanks to those responsible for making it available.

Mr Evans was born in Spencer Street, a stone's throw from the depot on Sutton Road. He obtained employment as a conductor in 1927 when Mr Dixon was the General Manager. After two and a half years conducting he became a driver. He was trained by another old driver, George Lewis and Mr Evans recalls, '*I remember him standing at my side on an open fronted tram, operating the controls and telling me what to do, until such time as I was able to take over for a distance. My training period lasted for six months and during the whole of that time I was also putting in about 70 hours a week as a conductor. I was passed as a driver by Chief Inspector Charlie Underwood, who after retiring, moved to Mablethorpe*'.

Mr Evans continues, '*I passed my test at the age of 20 years and 9 months, I told a bit of a fib because I told the manager I was 21; anyway, I passed my test and everything went well from there. In 1932 they changed over to buses and I learned bus driving on an old lorry of a furniture removal firm up Leeming Street to pass my bus driving test, which you had to pass before a Ministry of Transport official*'.

On the trams, the signing on time on the first car (if a man was on what was called 'the first Huthwaite') was 4.30am. That route (Huthwaite) served the colliery and also the CWS hosiery factory at Huthwaite. At that time of the day a workman's return was available up to 8.30am, but after that it was ordinary fare – from Mansfield to Huthwaite it was 5d. The other routes all served collieries except the Berry Hill route which was 1d from Mansfield Market to High Oakham school, the terminus. Woodhouse route served the Sherwood Colliery, Crown Farm served the Mansfield Colliery, Pleasley served Pleasley Colliery. That colliery, Mr Evans recalled, was the only one that was known to have men go down and work with ordinary candles – the other collieries had safety lamps.

The fares varied from one penny, the lowest, to five pence, the highest.

Uniform was a pair of trousers, green piped to match the colour of the trams, together with a tunic, again green piped, a great coat, a peaked cap and a cape similar to a policeman's. Men supplied their own boots and gloves. The latter were hardly a luxury because all the trams had open fronts – drivers would wear woollen gloves and scrounge old inner tubes from anyone breaking a car up. A covering would be made over the woollen gloves by sewing round the edge of the inner tube with string.

Under the tunic a driver would have to pack his chest with plenty of old newspaper against the cold. Sometimes in the winter, Mr Evans recalled, your eyelids became frozen and you would have to rub them with the home-made rubber gloves to free your eyelashes. The braking system he condemned as very, very poor. It consisted of a big brass handle which you had to wind on and on to make the brakes cling on to the wheels.

There was a 'sand hopper' under the driving seat with a sand pedal that when pressed ejected sand on to the rail. There was also a slipper brake, a block of wood which was wound on with a big handle, round like a wheel on to the rails. This was used mostly on Skerry Hill, coming from Crown Farm,

UEC car No.21 approaches the Red Lion loop on Stockwell Gate in the late 1920s. On the right is the recently erected Empire cinema. Photograph courtesy Mansfield Museum.

because on the car there might be 70 colliers (and more on occasions!). They would all be stood inside and clinging round the back on what they called 'the fender' and the driver wanted all the braking assistance that he could get. As Mr Evans said, 'you needed hand brake, slipper brake and plenty of sand because it was a very steep incline'.

People would pull the bell once to stop, anywhere, and they expected the tram to stop. There were no recognised stopping places – someone would announce, 'Will you stop at the yellow curtains, please', or 'Stop at that house with the white gate' and it could make life very difficult for the driver. There were of course recognised stopping places at all the loops but no doubt passengers 'tried it on' and some drivers were more obliging than others.

Mr Evans lived in Spencer Street from where it was two minutes walk to the tram sheds. Sometimes he would bring the last tram in from Huthwaite about half past eleven at night; living so near an Inspector would come round and bang on the front door and ask him to take the first trip to Pleasley (4.50am) as the rostered driver had 'missed'.

Mr Evans on the remuneration: *'Now I should like to say what my pay was, I think I started at nine pence an hour and I eventually got up to the top rate which was eleven pence an hour. Imagine that, eleven pence an hour. I used to do about 70 hours a week to be able to take home £2.00 and my wife, when it came to Thursday, always had half a crown left in her purse and she'd go down to the market and she'd bring a quarter of boiled ham, a small pork piece, a small loaf, two or three cakes and few more bits and bobs and perhaps come back with two pence change. With that two pence change, I could go and get five Woodbines and inside a packet of five Woodbines were two matches. So pay was very poor but perhaps with the cost of living at that time could have been considered fairly good and we had a decent living'.*

On the trams, Monday morning was the worst because it was cattle market day: *'You'd come from Huthwaite or you'd come from Pleasley or Woodhouse or Crown Farm or any other route into Mansfield Market and there would be people stood there with a crate of fowls, there might be another fellow with two or three rabbits, there might be another with some old wood he'd bought cheap on the cattle market and they'd all come and ask 'Can I put these in the front of the tram?' By the time you'd finished you'd hardly room to drive the car, there was so much stuff on the front platform'.*

Thursdays and Saturdays were busy because of the shoppers; they didn't put things on the front, they put them on the back where the conductor was. Mansfield before the Second World War had the fair in Mansfield market and there was no timetable

then. 'If you got into Mansfield at midnight from Huthwaite and thought "Right, this is my last trip, I'm going into the depot"' Mr Evans recounted, Chief Inspector Underwood would send you off again to Huthwaite. Off you'd go again, perhaps to Huthwaite with another load – the fair having to stop at midnight because of the music licence or some such thing: 'So people were knocking about till midnight and you'd got to take them back to Huthwaite'.

On the front of the car was what they called a 'cow catcher' (the 'lifeguard' mentioned in Chapter 8). Mr Evans described it thus: *'It was a tray underneath where you drove the car and right in front of the car was a gate made of lathes of wood built on a steel frame. And if anything hit that frame it would automatically make this tray drop on to the floor. So if anybody fell in front of the tram or any obstacle went in front of the tram it hit this gate and it allowed this tray then to drag on the floor. Very often they used to do this anyway when*

they were worn. If the attachments on the front were worn on the gate, the tray would drop and it would drag so you'd have to get out and pull it up again.

'Once on Pleasley, we got to Pleasley terminus, swung the trolley; I took the control lever to the front to drive back to Mansfield when a lady shouted to me "You've got a fowl there on your cowcatcher on your tray". And I had apparently picked that fowl up in West Gate somewhere and it rode all the way to Pleasley. So I let it stop on and give it a ride all the way back to Mansfield and then drove it off, I don't know where it went then'.

On the trams if a man wanted a bit of a holiday he knocked on the window at the offices and asked Mr Coleman (the traffic superintendent) if he could take a few days off. He'd shout back something like 'Yes, start on Sunday but you must be back Friday to start work on the Saturday'. Mr Evans never got a Saturday off, never had a Saturday holiday: *'The inspectors would put on you on Saturday nights on*

Huthwaite. Every tram was packed more or less when it got to late at night. Ten o'clock, half past and you're heading towards Mansfield Market, your heart would be in your mouth wondering if there would be an inspector there saying "OK, you must do another trip, these people have got to get back to Huthwaite"'.

There would be no timetable at all – twenty trams running, picking up, setting down, going into Mansfield and wondering when it got to half past eleven or so, whether to go back to Huthwaite. Nine times out of ten you would have to go back to Huthwaite: *'You'd pass a tram at the Red Lion passing loop (in Stockwell Gate) going back into Mansfield and you'd give him the sign that this was your last trip and he'd put his thumb up and burst out laughing at you and you'd got to go all the way to Huthwaite and back. Coming back from Huthwaite you'd perhaps have one on, one passenger. You'd ask him if he wouldn't mind walking into Mansfield to save you going down to market, coming back up Stockwell Gate into tram sheds to save yourself ten minutes perhaps. But ten to one he'd be an awkward passenger and he'd demand to be took to his destination'.* (Last trams from Huthwaite were in fact shown as terminating at the depot).

When the end of the trams came in 1932 Mr Evans was lucky – or unlucky – to drive the last tram to Huthwaite. The buses were due to take to the roads the following day on the Sunday. Mr Evans took his car to Huthwaite, came back to Mansfield market and got instructions from the inspector to drive on to the double track, the cinder track, which ran alongside Mansfield reservoir and then, presumably, to walk back to the depot. There were no flags flying and no celebrations to mark the occasion as was done later when the London trams stopped running.

'I wasn't pleased in one way to see the last of the trams and I wasn't really sorry; because when the buses came we had recognised stopping places and regular timetables and at night there was none of this another trip here, another trip there because people had to get back. All the buses stood in their respective starting off places. You'd stand by the bus and wait for a big blast on the whistle (from the Inspector) and that was the signal that every bus had to start then and that was its last journey and that was very different to the no timetable tram affair'.

Mr Evans went on to be a bus driver before being called up for military service in 1939, when he saw action in France, He came back from the Dunkirk beaches and went back again on D-Day, eventually crossing the Rhine into Germany. Mr Evans subsequently retired, but on the occasion of his 70th birthday he took over the controls of a tram again, after 50 years, when he was a guest of the National Tramway Museum.

Far left and left. **Car No.13 photographed by Mr Maurice O'Connor in Mansfield Market Place outside the old Moot Hall, then occupied by the Yorkshire Penny Bank. Maurice O'Connor, a Mansfield solicitor, was an enthusiastic recorder of the tramway scene in his home town and elsewhere and it is thanks to him that so many fine photographs of Mansfield's trams are available to us. This car is a Brush built model of 1906 with the short squared off roof. The roller blind destination boards have been replaced by detachable boards fitted to the side of the car. 'Post' advertisements were carried on the tops of many of Mansfield's trams. Other items of interest in the photographs are another sale of suits at the shop on the corner of the Market Place. Suit sales seem to have been very popular around this period (1930s). The top of the Bentinck Monument can be seen in the background. Photographs, Mansfield Museum.**

Open top car No.10 was one of the original Hurst, Nelson cars supplied in 1905. It remained in this condition until the end. Photographed in 1930 in Market Street, Mansfield. Photograph M J O'Connor, National Tramway Museum.

Brush car No.19, ex-Cavehill and Whitewell, in Stockwell Gate in the 1930s. The curvature of the bodywork (hogging) due to overloading, can be clearly seen. Photograph M J O'Connor, National Tramway Museum.

Chapter 11
Tramway Men and Women

I was very anxious, from the beginning of compiling this history, to include as much as I could find out about the men and women who made the trams work, whether as drivers, conductors, workshop, office or supervisory staff. I have included in Appendix A as many names of former staff as I have been able to trace, with as much about them as I have been able to find out. This I feel provides some social context to this history and also gives it a more human interest, as there are still descendants of former employees alive and well and living in Mansfield.

All the old staff have now passed on via that great tramway in the sky, but we do have a wonderful selection of memories recorded in the pages of the *Mansfield Chronicle and Advertiser* (*CHAD* to its friends). It is largely from these sources that much of the content of this chapter is derived and I am indebted to the *CHAD* for making these letters available.

In the previous chapter we read that Eric Evans was not too keen on the late turn to Huthwaite and most of his colleagues probably felt the same. However, not all the tramway men were glad to see the end of the trams. Many of them felt cut off as bus drivers in their little separate cab (this was before the days of front entrance buses) for as Edgar Jordan says in his book *The Tramways of Reading*: *'One feature of a tramway man's life, particularly on a relatively small system, was the way in which car crews became 'public figures'. The motormen on their open platform became known by sight to hundreds, possibly thousands, of people who saw them daily'.*

Arthur Plowright was one such Mansfield tram driver, having started in 1917 and because of his courtesy to other road users, he received a 'Knights of the Road' award from the *News of the World*. He was most upset when the trams stopped running and went back to being a conductor on the buses where he could remain in contact with the travelling public who he so much enjoyed serving.

John Wilfred Lamming came to Mansfield in 1914 from his native Lincolnshire. His father apparently knew Charlie Smith, who was at that time Chief Inspector on the trams and by fibbing about his age young John was taken on at the age of 14. After being trained for a month by two stalwarts, Fred Smith and Teddy Wear, he was taken on as a full time conductor. He was considered a 'smart young fellow' and the following year, at the age of 15, was detailed to train the first two lady conductors taken on by the company, Miss Elsie Carlisle and Miss Nellie Woodhouse. After a spell as a driver (at the age of 18) he was called up for military service and posted to India. On being demobbed in 1921 he was spotted by Joe Tranter, then the tramways traffic superintendent, in Mansfield Market and invited to return to work on the trams which he did a few weeks later. He remained a tram driver until their end in 1932, when he transferred to the buses and finished his career with the Midland General Omnibus company.

The highlight of Mr Lamming's career came in 1929 as he was driving

Workshop staff in the depot about 1910. The names of most of them are known. From left to right: John Gill, 'Tug' Wilson, unknown, Jock Taylor, Mr Skidmore and L Aves above, W Baguley, unknown boy, Mr Fisher, the blacksmith. The melodrama 'Greed of Gold' is advertised in the tram window at the Kings Theatre, Sutton. Photograph courtesy Mansfield Museum.

a Mansfield-bound tram along Outram Street, Sutton, when he was hailed by a Police Officer who had noticed a motor car being driven in an erratic manner. The officer instructed Mr Lamming to try to catch the car, which continued to zig zag across the road and the tram set off in pursuit. The officer then asked Mr Lamming to try to pass the car, so that he could stop it. However as the tram was accelerating to try to overtake the errant motorist, the car suddenly stopped in the middle of the road and the tram collided with the rear of it. The officer jumped off and went to the car door and Mr Lamming is reported as hearing him say to the driver 'Hullo my lad, what's your game?' The car driver, a well known local car dealer, was later charged with driving to the danger of the public and fined 5 guineas.

Mr Harry Witts was another employee, joining the company in 1910 at the age of 17. He was born in Mansfield and attended Rosemary Street school, starting work as a cleaner on nights at the Sutton Road sheds: *'I can honestly say that I did everything on the trams bar being an inspector or the manger; I worked on the overhead wires and I also helped to repair the tram tyres, great iron rings and with a gang on the roadway doing jobs like levelling the granite setts'.* His workmate was Bill Morland (W Vane Morland) who went on to be the manager of Leeds City Tramways in the 1930s.

Mr Witts as a cleaner was earning about 18 shillings a week when he got the chance to do a little relief conducting on the crowded Saturday night trams, and after two years he was made a full time conductor. His wages went up to 25-30 shillings a week depending on the number of hours worked. Two years later he qualified as a tram driver in the days when they were trained by such stalwarts as Charlie Underwood and Alf Cooke.

One event of his tramway service that he remembered was being on the first tram on the newly opened Crown Farm route in 1911, when he was delegated to look after the trolley rope on the trial run the day before the Board of Trade officials made their inspection. On this occasion, the driver was Joe Tranter, who later became Chief Inspector.

Despite his reserved occupation of tram driver, Mr Witts was called up for Army service in 1916. He had been engaged with others in teaching lady conductors how to drive as more and more men were being conscripted. One of these lady conductors tras Mrs Milly Plater, who was driving with several other women during the First World War.

Mrs Plater was born in Kensington, London, but later moved to Manchester where she married a Mr Frank Spittle. She came to Mansfield to work in

Mr Jeremiah Hooks at the controls of Hurst, Nelson car No.6. Mr Hooks was born in Norfolk and worked on the land scaring crows for a penny a week, so he was fond of telling his family. After a spell delivering mail by horse and cart he moved to Mansfield to earn his fortune in the coal mining industry. However, he preferred the open air life and joined the tramways and later worked on the railway. The back of this photograph has a note from Mr Hooks to his family in Norfolk. 'You should try this. It's like driving a horse with iron reins!' Photograph courtesy Mrs G Hooks.

domestic service which was one of the few jobs available to married women in those days and worked for a local colliery manager for some years.

When war broke out there was a call for women to do their bit and tram conducting was available as 'a suitable job for a woman'. Mrs Spittle as she then was, obtained a position as tram conductress, or 'lady tram conductor' as they were known.

She recalls: *'After little more than a fortnight I was trained to be a driver. I was nearly always on the Huthwaite run and often didn't finish work until round about midnight and then I had to set out and walk a couple of miles or so to Mansfield Woodhouse where I shared lodgings with some other women workmates in Priory Street. When I was on earlys I had to get up at three o'clock*

in the morning and set off from home to walk to Mansfield an hour later to be ready for a 5am start'.

Mrs Plater found no particular difficulty in learning to drive the trams. The real problem, she recalls, was negotiating the points and bends: *'The trolleys sometimes came off the overhead wires and the sparks began to fly then! The most awkward place for this to happen was in Mansfield Market place where the overhead wires crossed and recrossed those of the other routes'.*

Mrs Plater must have been a formidable lady: *'It wasn't very often that we had any trouble with passengers on the late night services who had too much to drink. If they refused to pay or were being awkward, the conductor used to fetch me. I knew how to persuade them to be sensible, and if they started swearing, I would swear back at them. They didn't like that – and it worked'.*

Women continued to work for the company for a number of years and in addition to Mrs Plater (or Spittle) there were a number of others including Miss Nellie Woodhouse, Miss Elsie Carlisle, a Mrs Stocks and a Mrs Oldham. There was also a Mrs Kynaston driving. She was known as the 'Gipsy Queen' to the locals, presumably on account of her black curly hair and ear rings. None of the women were ever allowed to drive unsupervised on the Crown Farm route owing to the heavy braking that was required when descending Skerry Hill with a car full of miners.

Women apparently had a far better deal from the Mansfield company than many women did in other towns. Southampton for example refused to employ any women at all and took on young boys as conductors until it was finally, grudgingly, accepted that women could do the job better, after the manager had been invited to visit neighbouring Portsmouth where women had been successfully employed for a number of years. Even then, Southampton would not employ women as drivers on the grounds that 'they were not considered to have the necessary physical strength or nerve power!'

Mansfield's embracing of female staff (not literally!) may have been due to the long-standing employment of women in local factories and mills together with one or two unfortunate incidents involving young male members of staff, in the early years of the First World War, which ended in Court proceedings.

On Saturday 9 May 1914, Edward Weir, aged 15 years, of 165 Westgate Lane, Mansfield was the conductor on the 11.20pm tram from the Market Place to Pleasley. While he was reversing the trolley the waiting crowd surged forward to board the car. He noticed one man climbing over the dash of the car to avoid the queue and, on requesting the man to get on the proper way, an argument ensued and Master Weir received several blows to the side of the head. The driver, John Hebbet of 19 Welman Terrace went to the assistance of his conductor but was prevented from doing so by the intervention of another man, a friend of the offender. Two Police Officers arrived and arrested two men. At the subsequent court hearing, the Chairman of the Magistrates said that if the Light Railway Company would insist on employing young boys, they must expect this sort of thing to happen! He dismissed the case against the man who had assaulted the conductor. The man who obstructed the driver was fined 10s 6d, presumably because the driver was an adult!

We have already read that female staff were more proficient at dealing with this type of incident. In a paper delivered to the Annual Meeting of the Transport Managers Association in 1916, the manager of the Greenock and Port Glasgow Tramway Company, Mr Archibald Robertson, had this to say about the employment of women as drivers: *'I believe the Greenock Tramways was one of the first, if not actually the first, to experiment with lady drivers and conductors* [in 1915] *not it will be readily understood from any desire to make a change but from absolute necessity'.* Mr Robertson went on to outline the training programme that he had successfully employed emphasising that the girls should be of 'good class' otherwise trouble was certain. He finished by recalling a number of occasions when, in an emergency, the lady driver had acted in every way correctly, stopped the car and then fainted away!

A Mr Hogg, who was chairman of the Sunderland District Tramways, said that they had 'very great diffidence' in starting women, as the line served a colliery district (as did the Mansfield system) and was very rough. The men went into town on Saturday night and when they came out they were very difficult to handle. However, the women were apparently used to dealing with men drunk or sober and as conductors they were a great success. They managed the men extremely well when the cars were very crowded on Saturdays. It was quite surprising what they had been able to do and when they first started 'they never believed it would be possible for women to cope with such traffic conditions'.

Perhaps Mr Hogg should not have felt so surprised. Most of the women would have been daughters, wives, sisters or even mothers of colliers and well used to dealing with their excesses.

D H Lawrence, the Nottinghamshire author, summed up their standing very well in his short story, *Tickets Please* set on the neighbouring Notts and Derby Tramway. The following extract is reproduced with permission: *'The girls are fearless young hussies. In their ugly blue uniforms, skirts up to their knees, shapeless old peaked caps on their heads, they have all the sang-froid of an old non-commissioned officer. With the tram packed with howling colliers, the lasses are perfectly at their ease. They pounce on youths who try to evade their ticket machines. They push men off at the end of their distance. They are not going to be done in the eye – not they. They fear nobody – and everybody fears them. They are peremptory, suspicious and ready to hit first. They can hold their own against ten thousand. The step of that tramcar is their Thermopylae.'*

Recruitment of women to take the place of men called up for active service during the First World War was generally organised locally, the government relying on local newspapers to arouse women's enthusiasm for such work. These campaigns it has to be said were haphazard affairs – many women recruited in Mansfield for example, had to find lodgings with the families of tramway employees, some having no homes of their own having been 'in service'. The mood of the country at that time was that women should be at home, raising children to replace those gallant men who had been killed in action, when the manpower situation 'at the front' was becoming serious. Even Sylvia Pankhurst, the suffragette leader, thought that tram driving 'was an unsuitable job for a woman'.

However, the introduction of women into transport started a 'mellowing' of the attitude of the hierarchy of that industry. 'Facilities' for ladies had to be provided and at tram termini, a local householder would be found willing to provide these necessities. The company would pay a small annual retainer, and toilets would be made available for tram crews. They were mostly outside in those days so the arrangement was not so awkward as it might seem nowadays.

On the late shift, tea and biscuits were provided, which was very much appreciated by the women. Whether or not these treats were provided for the men after the end of hostilities is not recorded! We do know however that then, as now, a hot cup of tea at the end of the line was always appreciated by both sexes.

Mr Robert Bedford at the controls of the Brush car No.18, with conductress Mrs Stocks, about 1918. Photograph courtesy Mrs Joan Sheldon.

Car No.5 stands in Mansfield Market Place about 1930. The conductor assists passengers to board as a baby Austin squeezes cautiously by. Note that the tram is about to move off on the offside track, en route to Nottingham Road. Tram No.5 was an extensive rebuild from one of the Hurst, Nelson open top cars. It was provided with a fully enclosed upper deck with four windows in each saloon. It had transverse upholstered seats on both decks, the only Mansfield tram to do so. The rebuild was completed in 1929, by which time the company had decided to replace the trams so no more were rebuilt. Nevertheless it was a fine piece of work for such a small workshop. The driver may be adjusting the controls, or he may be feeling in need of the product advertised over his head! Photograph Dr J Nichol, National Tramway Museum.

Chapter 12
The Last Years

In January 1923, Mansfield Corporation had indicated their intention of carrying out road widening works in Chesterfield Road near the Grammar school. The Tramway Company were prepared to double 1¼ miles of track in connection with these works, at a cost of £27,500 provided that the Corporation were prepared to make a contribution of £2,500. In April it was announced that the work had been agreed to and was expected to start in May. In the meantime, the overhead wire on the Pleasley route was renewed at a cost of £970.

Nothing further was heard until July 1924 when it was announced that a letter had been received from the Corporation stating that they would not be in a position to commence road widening works until the next year (1925).

The tramway company agreed to put off the doubling of the track until then so that the works could be conducted at the same time and a meeting was arranged with the Corporation to discuss arrangements. Meanwhile the Tramway Company placed an order for the necessary rails, in anticipation of the early commencement of these works.

In 1925 the company applied for further extensions of their lines, to

Forest Town, Rainworth and Blidworth. At the subsequent enquiry before the Light Railway Commissioners, it was stated on behalf of the company that they intended to order ten new tramcars to operate these services. The application was successful but for various reasons the new extensions were never built and the ten new trams never materialised. However, an order was placed on 23 June 1925 with the English Electric Co of Preston for two new trams. It is interesting to speculate whether or not all the ten cars proposed would have been of the same design.

We have copies of the order forms for these two cars and from them we learn that the cars were 15 feet 11 inches high and would therefore pass under the Mansfield Railway bridge on Nottingham Road (just!). The cars had the usual longitudinal wooden seats in the lower saloon for 28 passengers, with wooden garden type seats on the top deck for 46 passengers. There were no destination indicators but dioptric lens signal lights were specified with red, green and amber glasses. Hudson and Bowring life guards and Philipson side guards were fitted. Preston type folding steps and Preston sand boxes were specified, the latter with intermittent flow control.

They were also to have Peacock brakes, the operating gear consisting of a 10½ inch handle with a 20 inch slipper brake wheel. Preston pin and chain draw gear was also specified.

The trucks were Peckham P22 type with an eight foot wheelbase. The motors were BTH type 506A and the controllers type B510A. The order form specifies that the cars were to be of teak construction with 'special truss rod anchorages to be embodied'. The order having been approved on 2 October 1925 we may assume delivery some time after this date. These two cars were numbered 27 and 28 and were the last new trams ordered for Mansfield.

The company were obviously pleased with their new trams and set about rebuilding one of the old Hurst, Nelson cars to a similar specification. Car No.5 was taken into the Sutton Road workshops and emerged unrecognisable. Both saloons were rebuilt with four windows to each side and the upper deck was fully enclosed, although the vestibules remained open. Probably the greatest change was in the seating, which was fully upholstered and arranged transversely in both lower and upper saloons, the only tram in Mansfield fitted with rexine upholstered seating! The car was low enough to enable it to pass

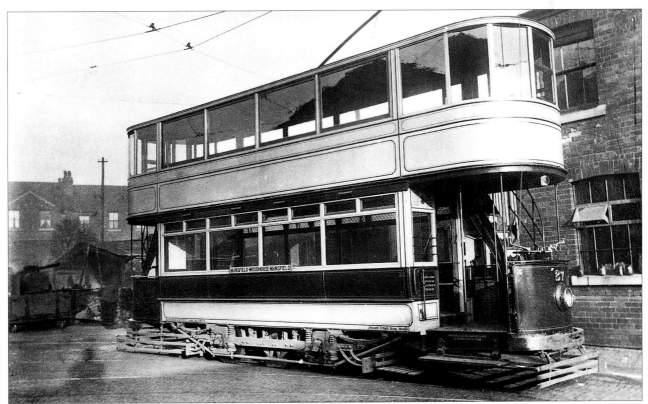

Newly delivered car No.27 outside the Sutton Road depot in 1925. This and sister car No.28 were the last two obtained by the company although there were plans to order ten of them from the English Electric Co. Photograph courtesy Mansfield Museum.

under the Nottingham Road railway bridge and it spent most of its remaining few years on that route.

Photographs of this car show that it was lettered 'Mansfield and District Traction Co' on the lower rocker panel, which appears to indicate that the car was not put into service until 1929, by which time the company had changed its name from 'Mansfield and District Light Railways'.

It is unfortunate that no further cars were rebuilt in this fashion. Many of them were in poor condition and numerous contemporary reports speak of excessive vibration, noise and lurching. Pronounced 'hogging' (sagging at the ends and a bowing up in the middle of the tram body) was apparent in many cars, especially the two Brush cars Nos.19 and 20. This was no doubt exacerbated in these two by the large numbers of passengers crammed in – there was seating, after all, for 72 passengers as against 47 on the earlier cars. The UEC cars and the 1906 Brush top covered cars had to be fitted with diagonal rods to counteract the lateral flexing of the bodywork.

A recent letter to the Editor of the local Mansfield newspaper CHAD recalls the time when the correspondent was thinking about leaving the coal mining industry to join the Royal Navy, back in the 1930s. A friend advised him to take a trip on a tram from Mansfield to Sutton and back and if he survived without being seasick, he would have no trouble at sea! The trams used to roll and pitch quite violently as they sped along the roadside track at the side of Sutton reservoir, which gave a nautical feeling to the journey. This was one of the few places that the trams could be opened up and they seemed to fly along, then down the hill into the town, with sparks flying from the wheels and overhead wires.

In 1925 arrangements were made for the loan of three cars from the Notts and Derby tramway, at a rent of £200 from 1 July to 31 December 1925. Three open top cars were delivered by road by a local fairground proprietor. These took the numbers 29-31 in the Mansfield fleet, but after a few months, Langley Mill sent an urgent request for the return of one of the cars and number 29 had to go back.

In July 1926 it was reported that the proposed meeting between the tramway company and Mansfield Corporation to discuss the road widening in Chesterfield Road had been cancelled yet again, at the request of the Corporation. The tramway company then gave up rand sold off the stock of rails.

In March 1927 at the Annual General meeting, the chairman Sir Joseph Niall made the following comments: *'Referring to the belief that the tramways were obsolete, the directors believe that they will continue to serve a useful purpose in supplying the travelling needs of the general public. More motor buses are being purchased, in order to supplement and assist the tramways'.* He also noted that the time for the completion of the tramway extensions to Rainworth, Blidworth and Clipstone had been extended for another two years, to 1 January 1929.

Despite Sir Joseph's words, he must have known that it was becoming impossible to consider extending the system; the 'infrastructure' (as we would call it now) of the tramway was so bad that the only solution would have been to build what was in effect a new system. There was neither the money nor the will even to consider this option.

Electricity was now being supplied to the town of Mansfield by the Notts and Derby Power Co, another Balfour Beatty subsidiary. This meant amongst other things that the Mansfield Corporation no longer had any interest in electric transport in the town. It also resulted in some unexpected problems for the tramway company, as in September 1928 for example when a steam boat was proceeding down the River Trent near Nottingham. The funnel of the vessel became caught up with the overhead supply cables and electricity to Mansfield was cut off, bringing the trams to a halt.

Competition for passengers between the tramway company and rival buses became intense. On the Huthwaite route there were 8 competing bus operators, on the Pleasley route 6 and on the Woodhouse route, 5. Despite fierce competition from private omnibus operators, 27 cars were needed to maintain the peak hour tram services. The Huthwaite line had a 7 minute headway requiring 10 cars, Pleasley a 6 minute service requiring 7 cars. Mansfield Woodhouse had a 9 minute service requiring 7 cars, Crown Farm a 15 minute service requiring 2 cars and Nottingham road a 20 minute service using just one car.

The bus operators also fought each other and local newspapers of the time are full of reports of the local Police taking action against bus men involved in accidents, racing, speeding and overloading offences. Indeed the position was worse than it had been in the days of horse drawn carriers competing with each other.

The Mayor of Mansfield, Councillor J A Beck, continued his scathing attacks on the tramway company. In his opinion, which was that of Mansfield Corporation, the trams had had their day and should be replaced by petrol buses. It was possible, he said, for a reasonably fit man to set off on foot from any of the tram termini and beat the trams in to town. He accused the company of being indifferent to the comfort of the travelling public. On Saturday night he had observed a tram crowded with people. It was pouring with rain and the tram was open top. No wonder the people referred the buses. In his opinion, the trams were only suitable for the old, the lame and the lazy. He admitted that the Corporation, who in those days were the Local Licensing Authority, had licensed motor buses to run in competition with the trams because in their opinion, the public were not getting the service from the trams that they were entitled to. This admission by the Mayor was described in the local press as 'an incredible and reckless policy.' There were at this time no less than 122 buses an hour entering and leaving Mansfield!

It is ironic that whilst the Mayor was propounding the virtues of motor buses, his Corporation were wringing their hands over the problem of ever increasing road accidents, many of which of course involved motor buses. As a result of the numerous cases now being heard by the Magistrates Court concerning offences by operators of motor buses, the Chairman of the Bench announced in July 1929 that heavier penalties would be introduced if offences continued at the same rate. Alderman Knapton, in reply, accused the Police of putting a telescope to their blind eye when trams were overcrowded. He had seen passengers 'clinging on like gnats' to a tramcar, yet if a bus was overloaded, the poor fellows were penalised. Alderman Bowles, noted for his outspokenness, commented if the 'Tramways Committee' wanted to know what was up with the trams, they should get out of their motor cars and try riding on them!

In January 1928 the long awaited meeting between the Corporation Highways Committee and the Tramway Company to discuss the road widening proposals in Chesterfield Road at last took place. The two sides were unable to come to terms over the relocation of the tram track and the single line remained on the west side of the road. This meant Mansfield bound trams had to be driven against the flow of traffic. The local state of economy was so bad, that the following extraordinary notice appeared in the Mansfield Reporter on Friday 30 March 1928:

'Mansfield and District Tramways Co Important Notice – Fares
Owing to the great amount of unemployment consequent upon trade depression in the district the company has decided to REDUCE THE FARES on all routes. The company will endeavour to continue these low charges until trade revives and if the public response justifies it, for an even

Car No.13 stands outside the depot in Sutton Road. Once the pride of the fleet, the vehicle now has a patched dash and has been fitted with diagonal struts on both decks, to counteract the flexing of the body work. Sic transit gloria tranvia! Photograph courtesy Mansfield Museum.

longer period. Without the co-operation of the public however the company may be reluctantly compelled to revert to the present charges.
M & DT Ltd
Sutton Road
Mansfield'.

In 1927, the neighbouring Notts and Derby Tramways Company had applied to Parliament for a bill permitting them to substitute trolley buses for trams over their route from Nottingham to Ripley. This Bill received Royal Assent in September 1928, the company was renamed the Notts and Derby Traction Co Ltd and full protection was given to the company against competition from private omnibus operators over its whole route.

In October 1928, no doubt encouraged by the success of their associated company, the directors of the Mansfield and District Tramways Company decided to promote a bill of their own, giving them the same powers, to substitute trolley buses or motor buses for the trams and to seek protection along the existing and proposed routes from private omnibus operators. They also sought a five year

period over which to effect the change. This Bill received Royal Assent on 10 May 1929. Unfortunately it did not give the Mansfield Company the same monopoly powers as the Notts and Derby Company had been given; moreover the period allowed for the changeover was reduced to two years. Nevertheless, Balfour, Beatty and Co were asked to prepare estimates for the change to trolley buses.

On 21 January 1929, Mansfield car No.26, one of the UEC balcony cars, was travelling along Huthwaite Road in thick fog, when it collided head on with a motor bus travelling in the opposite direction. The driver of the bus admitted that he had been following the tramlines because of the fog, but had not seen the approaching tramcar until it was too late. The bus swerved but became jammed between the tram and the overhead wire post.

The driver of the tram, George Sowter of 7 Shaftesbury Avenue, Bull Farm was uninjured, but the conductor, Francis Reginald Truscott was thrown to the ground as a result of the impact. The tramcar was a write-off and had to be scrapped as a result of this accident. Once again, the Notts and Derby tramway came to the rescue,

dispatching a covered top balcony car by road from Langley Mill. On arrival at Mansfield it took the number 29.

Meanwhile, in Mansfield, as elsewhere, road widening continued apace, permitting traffic to travel faster with the resulting increase in accidents. The Mayor himself was involved in a motor accident while returning from holiday in 1929 but like Mr Toad, his enthusiasm for the motor car was in no way diminished. But when the tramway company had applied to site the tracks for the proposed extensions at the side of the road so as not to hinder the traffic, the Corporation opposed this on the grounds that it would merely enable the trams to go faster. The Corporation insisted that all routes should be laid down the centre of the roads and that the roads should be widened to accommodate the tracks. At the tramway company's expense of course.

In December 1929 the manager Mr Dixon decided he had had enough and left to take up a post as manager of the City of Oxford Motor Services. He had been with the Mansfield company for ten years and was one of the few men to enter the Balfour, Beatty empire at managerial level from outside the organisation. He had started his engineering apprenticeship with the London, Brighton and South Coast Railway and completed it with Seimens Electrical. He served with the Royal Engineers in the South African wars, and in 1903 joined Hull Corporation Tramways. During World War I he served with the Royal Garrison Artillery, rising to the rank of Captain and receiving the Military Cross. On leaving Mansfield he was presented with a gold watch engraved 'A token of respect to R F Dixon Esq, from the staff and employees of Mansfield and District Tramways Co 1929.'

Mr Dixon was well regarded at Mansfield and had worked hard to bring the tramways up to date. One of the improvements brought about during his term of office was the founding of a Social Club and a wooden building was erected behind the tram sheds for various social events. The company also had its own football team who played on a field at Sutton Road opposite the tram sheds and Alf Cooke was one of the team members. His son, Reg Cooke recalls being sent by his mother to look for father one morning on his way to school at Moor Lane. His father had failed to return home after finishing his shift at midnight and young Reg eventually found him in the Social Club playing cards. 'He had been taking part in what you might call an all night session!'

recalls Mr Cooke junior. Mrs Cooke's thoughts on the matter are not recorded!

Mr Dixon was succeeded by Mr W W Clarke who had been manager at the Notts and Derbys tramways since 1924, having previously been manager with the Luton tramways, another Balfour, Beatty subsidiary.

Mr Clarke had gained experience working in the Electrical and Civil Engineers Department of Glasgow Corporation Tramways where his father had been Chief Engineer. He was later employed as a draughtsman for power and substation extensions and the design of rolling stock for Glasgow. After working for the Caledonian Railway, he spent six years as Assistant Engineer to the Lisbon Electric Tramways Ltd, a British owned company in Portugal. Returning to Britain he was employed as a Works Manager by Henderson's steam and electric crane manufacturers, before taking up employment with Balfour Beatty in Luton.

During this final period of tramway operation, the Huthwaite and Pleasley services were joined up to provide one through route. Up until then, all services had started from Mansfield Market Place, and as a result, congestion had become so serious that a resolution was passed by Mansfield Corporation to ban trams from stopping in the Market Place altogether. However, when it was pointed out that there had been no accidents involving tramcars for the past 20 years, the resolution was withdrawn! The problem was made worse by the practice of trams terminating on the nearside of the loop, then moving off in the opposite direction on the wrong side of the road. There seems to have been little

attempt at through running, which would have been possible with slight adjustments to the headways.

At a meeting of local councils in 1931 the company were pressed to abandon the trams quickly and substitute buses. At a further meeting on 12 November, the sum of £11,000 was made available for road reinstatement subsequent to the abandonment of the light railway.

Time was now running out for the trams. A board meeting on 27 June 1932 it was announced that an agreement had been reached with the AEC company to provide 40 new buses on hire purchase terms over a period of six years, at a total cost of £61,307. To accommodate the new vehicles, an extension to the depot was authorised at a cost of £3,500.

On Saturday 17 September 1932 the last cars made their way back from Huthwaite, Pleasley and Mansfield Woodhouse. On Sunday 9 October 1932 the last cars made their final journeys to Crown Farm and Nottingham Road.

In 1930 the following companies were reported to be operating motor buses in competition with the trams:

1. Sutton and Huthwaite route – Midland General, Trent Motor Traction, Naylors, South Normanston, Pratts, Pinxton Bus Co, Thompsons, Swaines, Porters.

2. Pleasley route – Trent Motor Traction, East Midland Motor Services, Ebor Bus Co, Robsons, Wardles, Clarkes.

3. Mansfield Woodhouse route – Ebor Bus Co, Baker Bros, Bevan and Bakers, Trumans, East Midland Motor Services.

No.28 in Mansfield Market Place near the foot of Leeming Street. This was the last new car purchased and arrived from English Electric's Preston works in 1925 with similar car No.27. They both had fully enclosed top decks but the driver's platform remained open. Photograph M J O'Connor, National Tramway Museum.

Chapter 13
Early Motor Buses

After the unfortunate experience of the 'Pioneer' steam bus, the next omnibuses did not appear until 1914. These were two 40hp Daimler petrol engine charabancs each weighing 5 tons with seating for 28 passengers, purchased by the tramway company to operate on outlying routes to Clipstone Camp and Warsop. On Friday 29 May 1914 the *Mansfield Advertiser* carried the following notice:

'On Saturday 30th May 1914, the Mansfield Tramways will commence a charabanc service from Mansfield to Warsop every Thursday and Saturday. The vehicles will be available on other days for private hire'.

Excursions were advertised to Ollerton for 2/6d and to Matlock for 3/6d, and a cover was available for use on wet days. The vehicles were evidently more successful than the Pioneer for within three months of entering service they had been requisitioned by the War Department and whisked off for duty elsewhere!

After the war, several more motor buses were purchased. In 1919, three Tilling-Stevens single deckers numbered AL 6613 to AL 6615 were obtained together with a Leyland AL 6840. More buses followed so that by 1927 the company was reported as

operating a fleet of two dozen vehicles, mostly Tilling-Stevens and Leylands, on services to Rainworth, Blidworth, Shirebrook, Warsop and later, to Southwell and Newark. The latter service was on behalf of the London, Midland and Scottish Railway which had formerly operated trains on that route.

To replace the trams, 45 new AEC Regent petrol engine double deck buses were obtained. In order to purchase these and to pay for removal of the tram track the company were obliged to obtain a considerable bank loan. The replacement took place in two stages. On Sunday 18 September 1932, buses replaced trams on the Pleasley, Mansfield, Woodhouse, Sutton and Huthwaite routes and on Monday 10 October 1932 buses took over on the Crown Farm and Berry Hill services.

There were no particular celebrations, although the event was recorded on camera, as the last two trams. No.6 still in its original open top condition, and No.28, the last tram purchased for Mansfield, posed with their crews at the Berry Hill (Nottingham Road) terminus together with one of the replacement omnibuses. The trams led the convoy out to the terminus for the last time, then the bus led the final procession back into

town. After the trams were withdrawn from service they were parked on the reserved track at the side of Sutton Road, opposite the reservoir, where they became an attraction for tramps and vandals as well as photographers. They were gradually dismantled and the bodies were to be seen in a number of gardens and allotments in the area. Two stood alongside the playing fields of the Brunts school for many years, believed to have been Nos.6 and 10.

The top deck from one of the UEC cars was in use as a summer house behind the Sir John Cockle public house in Sutton Road and another was to be seen for many years alongside the Pleasley to Teversal Road. There may be others and the author would be pleased to hear of them. An old Chesterfield tram was recently recovered in very poor state and has since been beautifully restored to working condition by the National Tramway Museum. It would be a marvellous achievement if the same could be done for an old Mansfield tram.

All this was not quite the end of the road for Mansfield trams. Representatives of Sunderland Corporation inspected the withdrawn cars on Sutton Road in 1932 and

'Omnibus triumphant' This was the impressive sight which greeted Mansfield residents in the Market Place, on the morning of Sunday 18 September 1932, when the first 17 new AEC Regent buses were lined up like an invading army, signifying the end of the tram system. The buses took over the Huthwaite, Pleasey and Woodhouse routes on that day, but the tracks in the foreground continued to be used by trams on the Berry Hill route for another month until the end of tram operations on 9 October of that year. Photograph Mansfield Museum.

purchased the bodies of Nos.27 and 28 for £45 each. These two then made the long journey north to Sunderland in 1933 where they were extensively rebuilt in the Corporation's workshops, becoming Nos.21 and 24 respectively in the Sunderland fleet. In this guise, both cars remained hard at work in their new home, with No.24 taking part in the final procession when trams were finally withdrawn from the streets of Sunderland on 1 October 1954.

Some years later, Balfour Beatty built a replica of an open top Mansfield tram which they used as a hospitality suite at various exhibitions and shows. The lower deck was fitted out as a bar and the upper deck with tables and chairs. The 'car' or should it be 'bar' was lettered 'Mansfield and District Tramways' and carried adverts for Mansfield Ales.

The final act of the tramways was played out in 1960, when a shopkeeper in Portland Square, Sutton, complained to the council about a rusty old pole outside his shop which didn't seem to do anything except obstruct the pavement. When the council

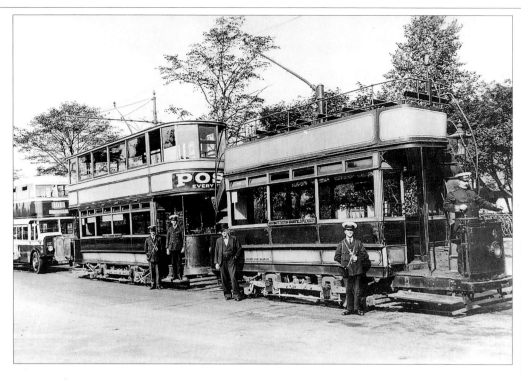

The last trams, after arrival at the Nottingham Road terminus. Car No.6, one of the original open top cars supplied by Hurst, Nelson and Co for the opening of the tramway, is in the lead. At the controls is Chief Inspector Charlie Underwood who had worked with the trams for 25 years. His conductor is D Moreton. Standing by in bowler hat and bow tie is Mr Coleman, the traffic superintendent. Next in line is car No.28, the last new car bought by the company in 1925. The driver is another long standing employee Mr Alf Cooke with B Groves as conductor. One of the shiny new buses, No.64, with B Marston driver and R Robinson, conductor, in their white coats prepare to take over the service. Photograph courtesy Mansfield Museum.

investigated, they found that the offending pole was the last overhead mast belonging to 'the tramways' and as such, nothing to do with them! After some inter departmental squabbling the pole was eventually removed.

The roles now reversed and the bus leads the procession back into town from the Nottingham road terminus on the last day of tram operation. 9 October 1932. Photograph courtesy Mansfield Museum.

Chapter 14
The Company and its Finances

The Mansfield and District Light Railway Company Limited was incorporated on 15 May 1901. It is interesting to follow its subsequent fortunes and finances by referring to the company's minutes during the years it was in operation. Messrs Chadburn, Manners, Robinson, Fish, Vallance and Hameyer were the first directors. However, difficulty was found in raising the necessary capital and in June 1903, the promoters sold out to other financiers and the Company was re-organised.

Mr Chadburn remained with Mr Wigley as the other local promoter. With Mr Henry Ruffer, a foreign banker, Mr Alfred R Holland, who had connections in the electrical and transport industries and Mr W McLaren, a financier, they formed the new board of directors. They were later joined by Messrs Fell and Kershaw.

In 1904, on Wednesday 2 November, at a meeting of the board it was announced that the Union of London and Smiths Bank were to be appointed bankers to the company. Mr Walker, the engineer in charge, was appointed General Manager and Secretary, to be paid £300 per annum. He was to furnish offices at Bentinck Chambers, Mansfield at a cost not to exceed £50. £4.15.6d was paid to the Midland Railway for the delivery and unloading of tramway rails at Mansfield.

On 5 January 1905 a letter was sent by Messrs Ashwell and Tutin, solicitors representing the company, to Mansfield Corporation, stating that 'Our clients are very disappointed at the delay in commencing work and are doing their utmost to induce the contractors to commence by the middle of the present month'. This was in response to a complaint by Mansfield Corporation about the slow progress of the works.

The Board meeting of 20 January 1905 was held in London. The Board heard that lease had been taken on land on Sutton Road, next to the King William IV public house, from a Mr John Beeston Hole, for the erection of car sheds. In February 1905 the Board expressed further concern at the slow progress of the works, and the engineer, Mr Walker, was asked to send a 'strong communication' to the contractors, J G White and Co. Whites, who were civil engineering contractors with various engineering interests, were a British subsidiary of an American company, with offices in Cannon Street, London. At the same Board meeting the sum of £15.6.8d was approved for payment for supply of punches and tickets, from the Bell Punch Co.

At the Board meeting of 2 August 1905 a month after the tramway opened, the Board heard that the manager had been pressing the contractors to put a second gang of men on the Sutton route and they had sent word promising to do so. It was resolved that the Sutton section should be completed with all possible speed and that it be extended to Hucknall (sic) in the least possible time. In the event, the Sutton section was opened on 19 December 1905 and the extension to Huthwaite on 17 February 1906, the latter being delayed by the need to lay iron girders to carry the tracks over the local council's sewage pipes.

On 12 September 1905 the Board received a claim from a Mr Kelly whose lorry had been damaged by colliding with one of the company's tramcars. The company's solicitors, Messrs Ashwell and Tutin were instructed to defend the action on behalf of the company. The Board also agreed to the placing of an order with the Brush Electrical Engineering Co of Loughborough, for a snow plough car. The company agreed to pay Mansfield Corporation the sum of 1¾d for the first 200,000 units of electricity and 1½d thereafter.

On 17 October 1905 the Board agreed to the tender by Mr Herbert Ashley of Mansfield, for the construction of a tramway along the new road (Yorke Street) on the Duke of Portland's estate at Mansfield Woodhouse. The sum of £1,578 was

Ex-Notts and Derby car No.30 stands in Stockwell Gate adjacent to the market, in 1932. Note the destination blinds fitted to this car. The original Mansfield cars had metal destination plates, carried on the sides of the car. Photograph M J O'Connor, National Tramway Museum.

agreed, subject to the Duke's approval. On 1 November 1905 the Board approved the arrangements for a parcels service to be provided by the company's cars. It was also agreed that Inspectors should get 7 days annual holiday with full pay after twelve month's service. The tender for 6 new cars from the Brush company, at a cost of £620 each was approved, as was the sum of £38 for a horse for Mr Chadburn.

Accounts presented for approval at the meeting on 15 January 1906 make interesting reading:

To Easterbrook, Allcard and Co (tools for smith): £7.3.10d

To W J Furse and Co, for wiring car sheds and sundries: £247.8.9d

To Miller and Co (wheel press): £80.0.0d

To British Westinghouse Co (motors and tools): £42.5.3d

To Bolckow, Vaughan and Co (rails and fishplates): £1000.0.0d

Mr H Ashley in respect of new road at Mansfield Woodhouse: £250.0.0d

Mr C R Walker, for trap and harness: £15.3.0d

To wages etc: £200.0.0d

On 19 February 1906 the Board heard that work was still not yet completed on the Mansfield Woodhouse route which was being constructed as far as Mansfield Woodhouse station (Midland Railway). Despite having had a favourable report on the agreement with the Bolsover Coal Co for the carriage of coal on the tramway, it was decided not to proceed with this proposal. The Mansfield Woodhouse route was completed soon after!

On 23 March 1906 the Board heard that Mr Kelly had refused the offer of £50.0.0d in respect of damage to his lorry and was demanding £80.0.0d. (He later accepted the £50 offered). They also heard from the company's accountants advising the allocation of funds to cover depreciation. A wise council indeed, but the company were not at that time in a position to accede to this suggestion.

On 27 June 1906 the Board received a demand from Mansfield Corporation for the sum of £300 in respect of electricity supplied, asking when they might expect the money. The Board decided, 'as soon as circumstances permitted' to make a regular weekly payment to the Corporation. They also heard that negotiations were taking place with the Corporation to try to get a reduction in the price of power.

On 10 July 1906 a letter was read from the contractors, J G White and Co, demanding that an outstanding account of £2,000 be settled, otherwise a writ would be issued. The Board agreed to send a cheque for the amount forthwith. Although not mentioned in the minutes of the meeting it was becoming obvious that the company

was getting desperately short of money. Mansfield Corporation had apparently made the right decision in not commissioning the construction of the tramways themselves.

As a result of the parlous state of the finances, it was decided to ask Mr A H Beatty, who was Company Secretary of J G White and Co, the contractors, to join the board of the tramway company, Mr Beatty having a reputation as a shrewd man of business. This was carried out with remarkable speed and Mr Beatty, who was later to make a considerable impact on the company's finances, took his seat on the Board at their next meeting, on 31 July 1906, three weeks after he had been threatening to take out a writ against the tramway company. One may surmise that the two events were not unconnected.

A Board meeting was called on 14 September 1906 to consider the implications of the tramway strike. Mr Beatty and Mr Chadburn were appointed as a sub committee of the Board, with full powers to deal with the strike question.

On 10 October Mr Walker, the tramway manager, was awarded £24 for his part in the settlement of the strike. A letter from the Brush Electrical Engineering Co of Loughborough, was received requesting settlement of their account! This was deferred until the meeting on Monday 26 November 1906, when Mr Beatty was appointed chairman, only four months after joining the company. This was not to the liking of some of the directors and a number of resignations followed, which were accepted 'with regret'.

Mr Beatty wasted no time in his efforts to get the company back into shape financially. The company's accountants were brought in to explain to the meeting the proposed arrangements for finance, by setting up a new holding company to be known as 'The Mansfield and District Tramways Ltd'. The new company would be responsible for raising finance, leaving the Light Railway Company to get on with its job of running the light railways, as required by statute.

Mr Beatty and Mr Chadburn then resigned their positions on the Board of the Light Railway Company. The ensuing vacancies on the Board were not to be filled – the new company was taking over and would acquire most of the shares of the Light Railway Co. No wonder a number of the old directors had resigned. One of the directors of the new company was Mr George Balfour, of whom more later.

The new company was formed on 7 December 1906. In March 1907, the first statutory meeting was held at the Market Chambers, Mansfield, with Mr A R Holland presiding. The chairman congratulated the new

company on being able to start on its career with an ample supply of money, not only enough to pay its way, but enough to feel it had an ample working capital to comfortably and conveniently carry on its business. The previous company (the light railway company) was never in that happy position. The report stated that the total receipts amounted to £73,319.15s and the payments to £70,717.11s, which included £68,823 for purchase of the shares of the Mansfield and District Light Railway Co. In seconding the report, Mr George Balfour said that the new company had really only just got properly on its feet, and when it settled down he thought it would be 'one of the best little tramway enterprises in the whole country'. At the next meeting of the Light Railway Company Board, there were only two directors in attendance, a Mr Wood and Mr Brown.

On 16 May 1907 the directors heard that arrangements had been made for carrying out a number of extensions and for the purchase of 4 new cars, a total cost of £9,300. On 26 November 1907 Mr Beatty reported to the Board that the extension to Mansfield Woodhouse had been completed and two 'new' cars were being delivered. These were in fact the two second-hand cars from the Cavehill and Whitewell tramway in Northern Ireland, but as the Board meetings were now being held in London, we may presume that the directors did not know where the cars came from. In March 1908, the second annual general meeting of Mansfield and District Tramways Limited was held, with Mr Holland presiding once more. A H Beatty, Geo Balfour, W A Plumbe, F Armstrong, W F Jolly, J Birch, J Butterworth, F Tudsbury, J Linney and C R Walker (secretary), were also present.

Mr Holland reported that the company was still not out of the woods, owing to having had to meet certain financial obligations (outstanding bills!) incurred by the Light Railway Company. He was happy to be able to report that such charges would not recur and a financial benefit may be anticipated in future accounts.

The accounts showed that the traffic receipts for 1907 amounted to £16,963.0s.5d and advertising rents etc to £349.14.10d making a total of £17,312.15s.3d. After allowing for traffic expenses, repairs and maintenance, power, insurance, rents, salaries and the rest the balance to be carried forward amounted to £8,052.9s.11d.

The payment of mortgages and shares amounted to £7,163.14s.9d, leaving a balance of £888.15s.2d. The chairman told the meeting that the Mansfield trams had carried 2,600,000 passengers of which 27,600 were workmen travelling at the workmen's rate. The cars themselves had travelled over 430,000 miles. He

Car No.24, built by the United Electric Car Co of Preston, stands in Mansfield Market Place in the late 1920s. In the background is the Town Hall, overlooking the bustle of the daily market. Photograph Mansfield Museum.

wondered how Mansfield had managed to get on with its business before the tramways were constructed.

At the general meeting the following year, 1909 with Mr Holland in the chair, and Messrs Balfour, Beatty, Chadburn, Birch, Butterworth, Richardson, Leman and Walker attending, the chairman was able to report that after paying a dividend of 6% on the cumulative preference shares, the balance on the year's working amounted to £2,138.3s.7d. The directors had been able to recommend at last the payment of £1,200 to a depreciation fund.

In 1909, Mr Beatty and Mr Balfour, who was also a director of the tramways at Broughty Ferry, Fife and Dumbarton in Scotland, formed their own company, Balfour, Beatty and Co Ltd. The new company quickly expanded and took over the Dartford and Luton tramways in 1909. The offices were always in London, latterly at 66 Queen Street.

This is not the place to go into history of Balfour, Beatty, but, of course, the company is still in existence today as a well known civil engineering organisation. On 16 February 1910 the proposals for the construction of the line to Crown Farm was approved by the two directors of the Mansfield and District Light Railway Company. The approved expenditure was £17,200 and the contract was of course awarded to Balfour, Beatty and Co.

The annual general meeting of the Mansfield and District Tramways in February 1911 heard from the chairman, Mr Holland, that the reserve

funds now stood at £6,212 and that during 1910, two and a half million ordinary passengers and half a million workmen had been conveyed. The tramcars had covered some 440,000 miles. These figures showed, he said, the magnitude of the tramways business that was being carried on.

In 1912 Messrs Balfour and Beatty set up a new company known as the Tramways, Light and Power Co Ltd, which in 1921 was renamed the Midland Counties Electric Supply Co Ltd. This company purchased the whole of the share capital of the Mansfield, Notts and Derby and Llanelly tramway companies. The entire share capital of the Light Railway Co was now owned by the Mansfield and District Tramways Limited, which became a subsidiary of The Midland Counties Electric Supply Co Ltd, which itself was owned by Balfour, Beatty and Co.

At the 1912 meeting of the Mansfield and District Tramways the directors were told by Mr Holland, the chairman, that over three and a half million passengers had been carried in 1911, and their cars had run over 500,000 miles. There was an available balance of £3,534.9s.5d, a dividend of 4% had been paid on the ordinary shares. The chairman congratulated the shareholders upon the improved financial position of the company.

In 1914 at the annual general meeting of the Mansfield and District Tramways the report to the directors shows a profit of £13,411.17s with a 5½% dividend payable to shareholders. It was reported that

during 1913, some 4,300,000 passengers were carried and cars had run an average of 10,500 miles per week. A reduction in the cost of electricity had been achieved, being for the first 400,000 units – 1¼d and 1d for every further unit. Meanwhile, the Mansfield and District Light Railway Company were continuing with their own meetings. The Minutes of the Meeting held on 8 May 1916 at the Mansfield office are typical:

'In attendance: Mr Holland, chairman, Mr Beatty and Mr C R Walker, secretary. The minutes of the last meeting were read, confirmed and signed.

The finances of the company showed credit of £10.13.4d (this figure remained unaltered for many years).

Signed A R Holland, chairman'.

The meeting was then closed, and directors retired to claim their hard earned fees. This entry is typical of the statutory meetings of the Light Railway Company Board. The company was still in existence because it had been set up by Act of Parliament, a 'statutory Company', but it now had no real powers. All the decisions were made by the Board of the Mansfield and District Tramways Limited, who were empowered to raise funds by methods outside the remit of the Light Railway Co. For example, they were permitted to operate motor buses, which the Light Railway Co were not. At the meeting of 28 January 1918 the sale of a 3 ton motor lorry to the Leicestershire and Warwickshire Electric Power Co for the sum of £600 was authorised and the purchase of a 'new' lorry from the Notts and Derby Co for £140 was authorised. This was the last meeting attended by Mr C R Walker in his capacity as secretary to the company.

In 1919, the sad death of Mr C R Walker was noted in the minutes. Also noted was the sale of the two cars to the Llanelly and District Tramways, for £1,020. In 1922, the death of Mr Chadburn was noted at the meeting of 27 June. Mr R F Dixon the new manager, attended the meeting for the first time. The purchase of a rail grinder for £360 was agreed and £43 was received from Mansfield Corporation as compensation for the failure of the electricity supply on 2 October 1921.

In 1925, at the annual general meeting of the Mansfield and District Tramways, the directors heard that the balance now amounted to £16,408.1s.10d and a 5% dividend had been paid on ordinary shares. These reports tend to show that the company was reasonably profitable during this period. However, 1926 was the year of the General Strike and the tramway suffered more than most during this period of industrial unrest, relying, as it did, heavily on the patronage of the coalfield workers. The strike seriously affected the financial position of the tramways and the report to the Board meeting in August 1926 presented gloomy reading. The earnings of the company were insufficient to warrant the payment of a dividend to shareholders and the effects of the strike, together with severe and unregulated competition from private motor bus operators, made it necessary to conserve the financial resources of the company. It also in effect killed off any hope that there might have been of building the extensions to Clipstone, Rainworth and Blidworth, which had been approved by the Light Railway commissioners

the previous year.

At the Annual General meeting of the Mansfield and District Tramways Limited in March 1927 Sir Joseph Niall DSO MP (appointed chairman July the year before) took the chair, Mr Holland having retired 'owing to advancing years'. Alfred R Holland had been associated with the Mansfield company as a director for many years, almost since its inception. Sir Joseph's report read as follows. 'Gentlemen, I very much regret that the company is presenting an unsatisfactory account for the first time in its history and is compelled to pass on both preferential and ordinary shares. This is due to motor bus competition and the low spending power of the public'. Sir Joseph went on to note that due to the effects of the strike, the Mansfield Corporation had had great difficulty in obtaining suitable fuel for their power station and as a result, the cost of electricity had also increased. It was also mentioned that the time allowed for the completion of the proposed extensions of the line had been extended for a further two years, until 1 January 1929. Despite the difficulties faced by the company, things improved slightly during 1928, so that the company were able to report a credit balance of £9563, enabling a dividend payout to shareholders and a balance of £3366 to be carried forward.

The meeting on Monday 8 October 1928 was a momentous one. The question of promoting a bill to authorise the replacement of the trams with trolley vehicles or motor buses was discussed, and at the same time changing the name of the company to 'The Mansfield and District Traction Company Limited'. The trolley bus routes were to be extended to Rainworth, Blidworth and Clipstone and at the same time the company sought protection on these routes from competing motor bus operators.

The matter was submitted to a

House of Lords Select Committee in 1929, where it was stated that competition from omnibus operators and the depression in the coal industry had brought the company within 'measurable distance of ruin'.

Eventually, the House of Lords Select Committee reported that it was prepared to recommend the provision of a protection order for the replacement vehicles on the existing light railway routes, but not on the proposed extensions. Also the routes must be converted within two years and not five as the company had requested. The Mansfield and District Traction Company Bill received Royal Assent in May 1929, and the company name was duly changed. Balfour, Beatty and Co were asked to prepare estimates for the conversion of the routes to trolley bus operation together with the extensions to Clipstone, Blidworth and Rainworth.

The passing of the first Road Traffic Act in 1930 was noted by the Board of Directors at their meeting of 8 October 1930. It was felt that due to the circumstances created by the passing of this Act the question of installing a trolley bus system should be postponed. In any case, the company had by now considerable experience in operating its motor bus services and the decision was therefore made to replace the trams with motor buses within the two year period. One gets the impression from reading these reports that the company had finally (and understandably) lost patience.

This effectively brought about the end of the Light Railway Company. Mansfield and District Tramways Limited continued until 1933 when it was renamed the Mansfield District Omnibus Company Limited and in 1937 it was reconstructed and amalgamated with the Traction company to form one company, the Mansfield District Traction Co Ltd. The old name lingered on however and even after the Second World War, the company and its buses were still referred to by the older generation as 't'Tramways'.

UEC car No.23 stands on the reserved track at the side of Sutton Road, after the withdrawal of tramway services in October 1932. Behind it stands one of the original Hurst, Nelson car, in unrebuilt condition. There is a wealth of detail to be seen, including the distortion of the bodywork of No.23 due to years of overloading. Photograph courtesy NTM.

Appendix

PERSONNEL

This is a list of names of some of the personnel who worked on the trams, with the approximate date of when they were serving. This is only a fraction of the total number of men and women who worked for the company, but these names have come to notice and are duly recorded hereunder.

Mr J Ackland, Assistant Manager/Engineer 1916

Harry Allaway, conductor of car from which passenger fell with fatal results 1908

L Aves Worksop foreman 1906

W Baguley, workshops 1906

Mr Beckett, driver, 1906

Robert Bedford, driver 1916

Jess Bickley, Insp 1918

Inspector Biddulph – took control of runaway tram, Stockwell Gate 1906

Mr Bowne, conductor 1906

George Brassington, driver 1918

Mr Butler, Inspector 1918

Herbert Butler, conductor 1928

Mr Cain, conductor 1906

Phoebe Carrol, conductress on runaway tram Stockwell Gate 1916

Reg Cardwell, driver/conductor 1919

Elsie Carlisle, conductress 1916

Mr Carter, driver 1906

Mr Chapman, conductor 1906

George Collins, driver 1920

Mr Colman, traffic superintendent 1930

Alf Cooke, driver 1916

Alf Cooke, workshops 1906

Charles Cooke

Mr Cooling, driver 1906

James William Crowder, driver – collided with cow on line 1916

W W Clarke, manager 1929

Mr Dellar, conductor 1906

R F Dixon, manager 1920-1929

Stanley Dudman assistant manager 1916

John William Edwards, driver 1928

Eric Arthur Evans, driver 1928

F A Fell, driver/conductor 1914 son of

Jack Fell, works foremen

C Fisher, workshops 1906

Mr Fryer, driver 1906

Christopher George, driver of car from which passenger fell Stockwell Gate 1908

Mr Gilbert, conductor 1906

J Gill, Workshops 1906

Mr Goddard, conductor 1906

Mr Graves, conductor 1906

B Groves, conductor 1932

Sidney Guilor, conductor on tram which collided with a cow 1916

John (Jack) Hammond, driver 1918

John C Harrison, driver of runaway tram, Stockwell Gate 1916

A Hawkins, conductor 1906

Mr Haynes, driver 1920

J Hebbet, driver 1914

Jeremiah Hooks, driver 1906-1914

W Hopewell, Inspector on tram from which passenger fell Stockwell Gate, 1908

Mr Kitchen, conductor 1906

Mrs Kynaston, conductress/driver 1916

John Wilfred Lamming, driver/conductor 1915

Mr Lammin, driver 1906

George Lewis, driver 1927

Bill Lomas, Inspector 1914

Mr Malt, driver 1906

Mr Mayman, conductor 1906

D Moreton, conductor 1932

William Vane Morland, workshops/driver, 1906. Later Captain Morland, manager at Walsall, Notts and Derby trams and Leeds Corporation, 1932-1945

Mr Neville, driver 1906

Mrs Oldham conductress 1916

Michael O'Reilly. Inspector on tram from which passenger fell 1908

J Overton conductor 1912-on runaway tram

Mr Peet, conductor 1906

George Parker, driver 1911 – famous for his walrus moustache!

Mr Parkes, driver 1906

Arthur Pilkington, driver 1912 – driver of runaway tram, Skerry Hill 1912

Mrs Milly Plater formerly Spittle, conductress/driver 1916

Arthur Plowright, conductor/driver 1917 'Knight of the Road'

Ivor Redvers Rabbits driver/conductor 1930

Jimmy Rabbits, driver 1918

Freddy Rabbits, driver 1930

L Radford, workshops 1906

Charles Revill. Inspector – on runaway tram Skerry Hill 1912

Mr Richardson driver 1906

Inspector Thomas Riding. Collapsed and died at work 1927 from effects of flu'

William Shepperson, driver 1906 – driver of runaway tram, Stockwell Gate 1906

Mr Skidmore, workshops 1906

Charles Smith, conductor 1906, Chief Inspector 1914

Edward William Smith, conductor 1905

F Smith, driver/conductor 1914

H Smith, conductor 1906

George Souter, driver 1924

Mr Spinks, conductor 1906

Mr Starham, driver 1906

Arthur Stevens, conductor

Fred Stevens, driver 1920

Mrs Stocks, conductress 1918

Mr Charles R Tatham, driver 1906, engineer/acting manager 1919

Jock Taylor, workshops 1906

Mr Thompson, conductor 1906

Mr Topman, conductor 1906

Joe Tranter, Traffic Superintendent 1930

Mr Truman, driver 1906

Francis Truscott, conductor 1929

Charles Underwood, driver 1906. Chief Inspector 1930

George Waterfield 1918

Charles Robert Walker, engineer, secretary and manager 1905-1916

Vernon Watson

Edward 'Teddy' Wear, driver/conductor 1914

Edward Weir, conductor 1914

Tug Wilson, workshops 1906

Mr Williams, driver 1906

Harry Witts, driver/conductor 1915

Miss Nellie Woodhouse, conductress 1916

Mr Wootton, driver 1906

Mr Wright, driver 1906

TIMETABLES

At the opening of the tramways in July 1905, the following provisional timetable was in force.

The first car left the Market Place for Pleasley Hill at 4.45am and continued half hourly until 7am, after which the service was every 15 minutes. The last car left the Market Place for Pleasley at 11pm. From Pleasley the last car left for Nottingham Road at 10.35pm, for the Market Place only at 11.20pm and from the Market Place to Nottingham Road, at 10.55pm, this being the 10.35pm car from Pleasley. On Sundays, the first car left the Market Place for Pleasley at 9.40am and the last at 10.10pm. The last car from Pleasley for Nottingham Road was 10pm and for the Market only, 10.30pm. From Nottingham Road the last departure on Sunday was 10pm, from the Market 10.10pm, arriving at Pleasley 10.20pm.

By September 1905, the service had been revised. The first car for Pleasley now left the Market at 5.15am, then at 5.40, 6.20, 7.5, 7.45, 8.15am, then every 15 minutes until 10.30pm (Saturdays 11.15pm). Services left Pleasley for Mansfield at 6.0am, 6.40, 7.25, 8.5, 8.35, 8.50am, then every 15 minutes until 10.50pm (Saturdays 11.35pm). On the Nottingham Road route, a 15 minute service was provided commencing at 8.10am from the Market and 8.20am from Nottingham Road. The last car left the Market at 10pm for Nottingham Road, (Saturday at 11pm), returning at 10.10pm, (Saturdays 11.10pm).

By 1908, the routes to Sutton, Huthwaite and Mansfield Woodhouse were up and running and the timetable for that year shows that the journey time for Sutton was approximately 22 minutes and the full trip to Huthwaite, 35 minutes. On the Mansfield Woodhouse line, the journey time was 12 minutes. On the Pleasley route the journey time was 17 minutes. Through running to Nottingham Road had now ceased and the journey time on that line was approximately 7 minutes.

The timetable for 1928 shows the first car from Mansfield to Huthwaite at 4.45am, thence every 30 minutes until 6.45am, then every 15 minutes until 11.05pm. On Sundays the first car left the Market at 9.30am then every 15 minutes until 5.00pm. After that there was a 12 minute service until 10.05, with the last car at 10.35pm. On the Mansfield Woodhouse route, the first car left at 5.51am, then every 15 minutes until 5.00pm. There was a 10 minute service until 8.30pm, then every 15 minutes. The last car was at 11.05pm, returning from Woodhouse 15 minutes later. On Sundays the first car left at 9.45am and the last at 10.35pm. On the Crown Farm route, the first car left the Market at 5.15am, then every 15 minutes until 11.05pm.

Apparently reflecting the heavy use of the line by work people, the first car on Sunday to Crown Farm was not until 12 noon, with the last car leaving at 10.35pm. The first car for Nottingham Road (Berry Hill Lane) left the Market at 8am, returning at 8.10am, then every 20 minutes until 10.05pm. On Saturday the last car left at 11.05pm returning at 11.15pm. On the Pleasley route, the first car left at 4.50am then every 20 minutes until 9.00am. After that was a 12 minute service until 9.48pm. then at 10.05, 10.20, 10.35, 10.50 and the last car left at 11.05pm returning from Pleasley 20 minutes later. On Sunday the last car left the Market at 10.35pm.

In 1929, amendments to the timetable were recommended by the Inspectors to the manager Mr Clarke, due to the market closing earlier and theatre and cinema performances being over by 9.00pm. The recommendations showed a saving on the numbers of cars needed to operate the services. It also meant that the Huthwaite and Pleasley services could be operated as one through service and the open top cars could be left in the sheds, except at very busy times. There were at this time still 10 open top cars in service and 27 cars were needed to maintain the existing service at peak periods. According to Eric Evans, the cars continued to run at night until all the crowds had been cleared. This was not unusual and occasionally the power was cut off before the last car had returned, requiring a hasty telephone call from the crew!

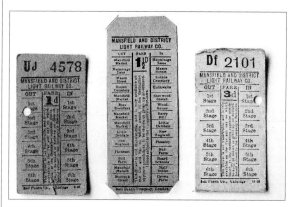

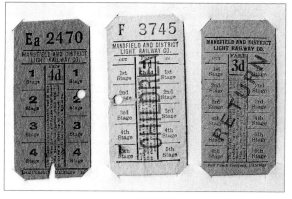

TICKETS

Tickets were of the normal Bell Punch type clipped into a wooden rack which the conductor held in one hand, whilst on a leather strap worn over the shoulder was carried the Bell Punch machine. Tickets were punched by the machine at the appropriate Stage, and the small circle punched out (confetti) was carried inside the machine to be counted up in case of a discrepancy in the takings. The machine rang a bell when it punched the ticket so that the passenger knew that the ticket had been correctly issued.

The first tickets recorded were ticket A0000 which was issued to the Mayor of Mansfield on the inaugural trip on 5 July 1905, A0001 to the Deputy Mayor, A0002 to the Mayor's Lady, A0003 to Mrs Alcock and A0004 to the local 'Advertiser' representative.

Mansfield tram tickets are very scarce. However, the examples above and on the cover are housed in the Mansfield Museum.

1d ordinary, in red, with six numbered stages.

1d children's ticket, in white, with 5 numbered stages and overstamped CHILDREN in red.

1½d ordinary, in blue. This ticket was 3 inches long and marked with 7 named stages.

2d ordinary in pink with 6 numbered stages; reverse advertises 'Stephens Ink'.

2d workpeople's return in buff with named stages, overstamped RETURN in red and marked with a large purple figure like an 8; reverse advert reads 'Be sure to ask your Grocer for Keene's delicious table jellies and creamy custards.'

3d ordinary in buff, with 6 numbered stages; reverse advertises 'Hardy's Starlight in bottle.'

3d yellow, overstamped RETURN in red.

4d ordinary in orange, with 4 numbered stages.

There is also a 6d pink, with days of the week across the top and marked Mansfield Market on the left and Huthwaite on the right. Overstamped RETURN in red.

Unfortunately, no 5d ticket has so far come to light.

There are similar tickets headed 'Mansfield and District Tramways Ltd'. Confusingly, these were issued on the company's buses.

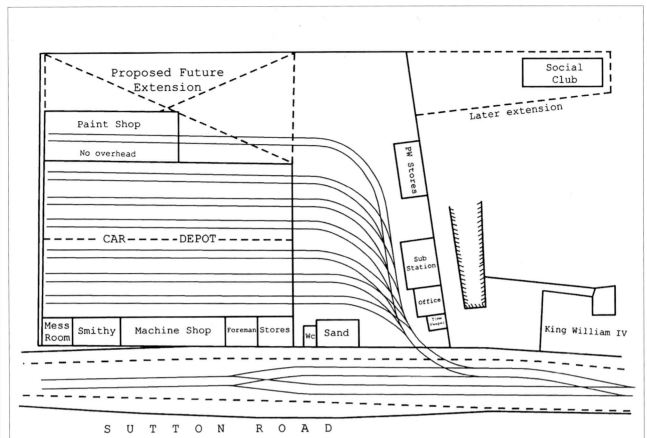

SITE PLAN

Car Departure Points Mansfield Market Place

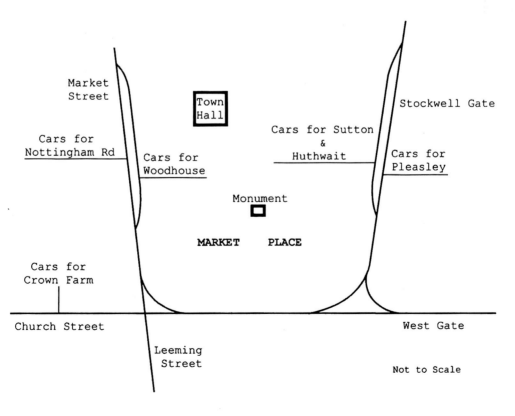

FARES

At the opening of the service in 1905, the proposed fares were listed in the Mansfield Reporter newspaper.

'One Penny': Pleasley and Toll Bar, Toll Bar and Bould Street (Chesterfield Road), Bould Street and Market Place, Market Place and Berry Hill Lane.

'Twopenny': Pleasley to Bould Street, Toll Bar to Market Place, Bould Street to Berry Hill Lane.

'Threepenny': Pleasley to the Market Place.

By September the fares had been revised as follows: Between Pleasley and Pump House – 1d, Pump House to Mansfield Market – 1d, Mansfield Market to Nottingham Road (Berry Hill Lane) – 1d, Norfolk Drive to St Mark's Church – 1d, Pleasley terminus to Mansfield Market – 2d, Pump House to Berry Hill Lane – 2d, Berry Hill Lane to Pleasley – 3d.

Children's Fares were shown as follows: children in arms under 3 years of age – Free, Over 3 and under 12 years of age – Two penny stages for 1d, beyond two stages 2d.

Workpeople Fares: Between Pleasley and Mansfield Market – 1d, Pump House to Berry Hill Lane – 1d, Pleasley to Berry Hill Lane – 1½d. These tickets were only to be issued on Ordinary Cars before 8am and on certain Cars between 4 and 7pm.

Ordinary Tickets were available in packets of 13 for 1s, Workmen's Tickets in packets of 12 for 1s, Scholars' Tickets in packets of 12 for 6d could be purchased 'on application to the Manager's Office, the Depot (Stockwell Gate) or from the Inspectors'.

'Tickets are not transferable and are available for one journey only on the Car on which they were issued. They must be produced for inspection on demand. Special Cars for Private Parties, Picnics, School Treats etc can be arranged for by giving a few hours notice to the Manager, from whom terms may be had on application. Cars stop to pick up or set down Passengers only at places indicated by Tablets attached to the Poles. All complaints to be made in writing to the Manager.'

Proposals were made to increase fares in 1918, when the following fare stages were in operation. The proposed increases were approved during 1919:
Market to Berry Hill – 1d.

On the Crown Farm route: Market to Bentinck Street – 1d, Bentinck St to Crown Farm – 1d, Market to Crown Farm – 1½d.

On the Woodhouse route: Market to Sherwood Street bottom – 1d, Borough boundary to Woodhouse terminus – 1d, Market to Woodhouse terminus – 1½d.

On the Pleasley route: Market to Debdale Lane – 2d, Debdale Lane to Pleasley – 2d, Market to Pleasley – 3d.

On the Huthwaite route: Market to Hermitage Lane – 1d, Hermitage Lane to Mason Street – 1d, Mason Street to Sutton Cemetery – 1d, Sutton Cemetery to Huthwaite – 1d, Market to Mason Street – 1½d, Hermitage Lane to Sutton Cemetery – 1½d, Mason Street to Huthwaite – 1½d, Market to Sutton Cemetery – 3d, Hermitage Lane to Huthwaite – 3d, Market to Huthwaite – 4d.

Under the proposals, the 1d fare would be increased to 1½d, the 1½d fare to 2d, the 2d fare to 3d, the 3d fare to 4d and the 4d fare to 5d.

In July 1925, the following notice appeared in the Mansfield Advertiser;
'1d STAGES
On and after Monday, July 20th, 1d. Tickets will be issued between the following Stages:
SUTTON AND HUTHWAITE ROUTE
Mansfield Market and Moor Lane
Moor Lane and Kings Mill
Kings Mill and Skegby Lane, Sutton
Skegby Lane and Portland Square
Portland Square and Jubilee Cottages
Jubilee Cottages and Huthwaite Terminus

PLEASLEY ROUTE
Market Place and Pheasant
Pheasant and Shaftesbury Avenue
Shaftesbury Avenue and New England
New England and Pleasley Terminus

WOODHOUSE ROUTE
Mansfield Market and Park Avenue
Station Street and Terminus

CROWN FARM
Mansfield Market and Bentinck Street
Bentinck Street and Hall Street
Hall Street and Terminus
No Children's Half Fares will be issued
The Management reserve the right to cancel or alter the arrangement without notice.'

These fares remained in force until April 1928 when, due to the trade depression and unemployment in the area, the fares were reduced to their original level.

PARCELS

The Light Railway Company operated a Parcels Express service, whereby parcels could be collected and delivered to within half a mile of the Company's lines and terminii, from offices along various parts of the lines.
The central office was at Carr's Boot Shop in Mansfield Market and other agents were:
Mr Straw, Forest Side Potteries, Sutton
Mr Bristol, Outram Street, Sutton
Mr Dickens, Sutton Road, Huthwaite
Mr Burgess, Sherwood Street, Woodhouse
Mr Marsh, Tram Terminus, Woodhouse
Mr Wright, Mansfield Road, Pleasley

PASSENGERS

In 1906, it was reported that 2,000,000 passengers were carried. In 1914, the number was 4,400,000 and buses are recorded for the first time as having carried 1,200 passengers. In 1919, the trams carried 7,500,000 passengers but by 1925, this had dropped to 6,000,000. Buses are shown in this year as carrying 1,000,000 passengers. In

1930, the trams carried 5,600,000 passengers and the buses 2,000,000. In 1931, the last full year of operation, the trams carried 5,150,000 passengers. The average number of passengers carried, and mileage run per week, during the last two full years of operation were as follows:
HUTHWAITE
1930: 28,746. Miles run by cars=4,747
1931: 24,535. Miles run by cars=4,910
PLEASLEY
1930: 25,291. Miles run by cars=3,444
1931: 23,145. Miles run by cars=3,006
WOODHOUSE
1930: 24,027. Miles run by cars=2,054
1931: 19,360. Miles run by cars=2,320
CROWN FARM
1930: 22,805. Miles run by cars=1,698
1931: 20,768. Miles run by cars=1,677
NOTTINGHAM ROAD
1930: 12,025. Miles run by cars=664
1931: 11,409. Miles run by cars=700